Gardening

Can Be Fun

Stuart Jackson

Title Page:
Mesembryanthemums—a beautiful splash of summer colour.

Photographs:

Cover © Sheffield Newspapers Limited
● © Stuart Jackson
＊ © Sheffield Newspapers Limited
† © Phil Butcher Photography
‡ © Harry Smith horticultural photographic collection
All others Pat Whitehead— ©The Hallamshire Press

Text and design © 1996 The Hallamshire Press

Published by The Hallamshire Press
The Hallamshire Press is an Imprint of
Interleaf Productions Limited
Broom Hall
8–10 Broomhall Road
Sheffield S10 2DR
England

Typeset by Interleaf Productions Limited
Printed in Spain by Edelvives

British Library Cataloguing in Publication Data
A catalogue record for this book is available from the British Library

ISBN 1-874718-18-0

Foreword

GARDENING AND RADIO seem to be made for each other. Long before I became seriously interested in gardening myself I started listening to BBC's *Gardener's Question Time* and became a fan of Fred Loads and Bill Sowerbutts who, with names like that, could only have been gardeners. They talked about plants as though they were members of the family. Then, when my own garden began to fascinate me, I could truly share in the grief of somebody who had lost a camellia after years of tender loving care.

There is something about gardening that makes a person into a philosopher who, as well as having green fingers and expertise, also dispenses earthy wisdom and waspish humour. Sowerbutts, Loads, Geoffrey Smith, Percy Thrower and Geoff Hamilton they all possessed the ability to be entertaining as well as enlightening. BBC Radio Sheffield's Stuart Jackson comes from the same root stock, earthy, chatty, full of aphorisms and quirky folk-lore and above all — good advice. A few years ago I moved house and inherited two beautiful azaleas. The first year they were a mass of flowers, the second year nothing! 'Frost' said one expert. 'Old-age', said another. 'It wants some iron', said Stuart Jackson. He was right. A few doses of trace elements and the azaleas bloomed as well as ever they had. Multiply my experience by thousands of other listeners and you can understand why he has become so popular in South Yorkshire. Stuart thinks gardening is a fun subject but it ceases to be so if your efforts are never rewarded with good end products. This book will help your garden grow and increase your fun at the same time. Away with canker, blight and blossom drop, with Stuart Jackson to help you the good times are waiting round the corner.

Jack Shaw
BBC Radio Sheffield's
Sunday Morning Breakfast Show

An exotic plant in the author's garden—Angel's Trumpets (Datura Sanguinea).

Contents

The author reaping a harvest of raspberries. *

Introduction

THE FOLLOWING PAGES are the result of a lifetime of gardening, plus a fair amount of gentle encouragement from many people—not least of whom are the many callers to my weekly gardening broadcast for BBC Radio Sheffield and the audiences of my garden talks and lectures.

When I look back I realise how lucky I have been, for, as I've often been heard to comment, my job's my hobby and my hobby's my job. I have been fortunate enough to have spent many years employed in gardening (or, to give it its Sunday name, 'horticulture'), and to have spent my spare time growing, showing and broadcasting.

As radio listeners will know, one of my often-repeated phrases is 'Gardening's a fun subject, so let's have fun!' I have always found gardening so therapeutic—nothing relieves the stress of a hard day better than unwinding in one's own garden.

Nature is a perverse creature; we can assist and perhaps even mould her, but in the end she will do her own thing. Yet surely in this lies the challenge of gardening: for if everything went exactly as we planned, we'd lose most of the fun and excitement.

Gardening can be compared to painting the Forth Bridge: when the painters reach the end they return to the other side and start again. Gardening too is an unending process—but it is more than just a task; it is a love.

I feel the following aptly sums up far better than I the theme of this book:-

If you would be happy for a week,
Take a wife.
If you would be happy for a month,
Kill a pig.
But if you would be happy all of your life,
Plant a garden.

Old Chinese Proverb.

Stuart Jackson

The author in his garden.†

Soil

*To dig one's own spade into one's own earth! Has life
anything better to offer than this!*

Beverley Nichols

JUST AS PLANTS are constantly changing, so is the soil in which
they grow. Both are living organisms, and knowledge of this is the
key to success. All soils can be improved, and it is essential to
remember that each crop and season alters the soil, sometimes
dramatically. Naturally, the garden's location dictates the soil type,
from heavy clay to light sand, and each has its own peculiarities and
pluses and minuses. To be successful we must understand the kind
of soil we are dealing with, and act appropriately. Although delving
into the intricacies of soil chemistry might seem highly technical,
we shouldn't ignore it, as soil preparation is vital to success.

Soil should have the following key properties:

1. It should be friable, so that seedlings and tiny roots can
   permeate easily.
2. It should be free-draining, yet at the same time be
   moisture-retentive.

Although one sounds like a contradiction of the other, what we
are trying to achieve is a balance between the two: soil needs to be
free-draining so that roots are not standing permanently in water,
but we must also remember that all nutrients can only be taken up
in a liquid state. When we apply fertiliser in granular or powder
form, these can only be absorbed or taken up by the roots in a
soluble form.

3. Plant roots must breathe (oxygen is vital to roots), so
   hard compaction should be avoided at all cost, as should
   persistent saturation.

New gardeners often get confused when we talk of planting shrubs
and the like very firmly. 'Is this not destroying the *breatheability* of
the soil?' they ask. The simple answer is that this wonderful

substance we call soil is made up of millions of crumbs, all odd shapes, which have vast numbers of air galleries or passageways running between them. This is the reason for incorporating grit or sand into very heavy clay soils: it opens them up and allows them to breathe.

SOIL TYPES

Light sandy soils have the advantage of being 'early' soils, i.e. easy to break down to a fine tilth, so they are ideal for seed sowing. They warm up much more quickly, but have the disadvantage of being so free-draining that nutrients are easily washed away, and this type of soil also suffers badly in drought conditions.

Heavy clay-type soils, on the other hand, have the disadvantage of being slow to warm up and have a large crumb structure, which is difficult to break down to a fine tilth. However, this type of soil is less affected by drought conditions, being more water-retentive and normally richer in nutrients.

A balance somewhere between the two types is the ideal—a loamy soil with a good crumb texture that is easily worked, rich in nutrients, drought-resistant, free-draining yet water-retentive. This is an ideal that you're unlikely to find, but it's what we're aiming for.

Clay soils can only be improved by working them, so elbow grease is called for here. Nothing improves the texture of a clay soil more than digging and growing a crop. Long strawy manure is a great help in opening up or 'flocculating' the structure. Grit or grit sand is also helpful, *but not builders' sand*. Gypsum is the main ingredient of most commercially available 'clay breakers', but you will need to add sulphur to adjust the pH—more on this later. Similarly, on light sandy soils, garden compost, animal manures (our old friend the horse) will help to bulk up the structure and improve moisture retention.

HUMUS

We now come to the two most essential facts about soil, namely pH and the magic word humus.

Humus is a complex subject, perhaps best introduced by quoting the *Oxford English Dictionary*:

> **humus**, n. Vegetable mould; the dark-brown or black substance resulting from the slow decomposition and oxidation of organic matter on or near the surface of the earth, which . . . forms the soil in which plants grow.

Although this sounds quite a mouthful, humus is, in short, the basis of plant fertility. An understanding of humus and its sources is the key to becoming a real gardener. It truly is a magic ingredient, and means the difference between success and failure. A humus-rich soil is one that is amenable to plant roots, that is moisture-retentive yet free-draining, and when fertilisers are added to this kind of soil they will *feed the plants and not the soil*. Soils that lack humus will utilise fertilisers to enrich themselves and not the plants.

So where do we obtain this 'magic potion'? Listed in order of importance, I suggest the following sources.

*Effort put into the condition of your soil pays dividends.**

1. Garden Compost

No self-respecting gardener should be without a compost heap, irrespective of how small the garden. Much has been written on the subject of garden compost, so it should suffice for me to make a few salient points.

The most obvious site for the compost heap is a spare corner of the garden—ideally under a tree, against a wall, behind a garage or outhouse—directly onto the ground. For neatness, this can be contained by constructing a small fence from chicken wire and posts.

All organic material can be added to your compost heap: annual weeds, light prunings and kitchen waste of a vegetative nature. Don't forget to include teabags, eggshells (a superb source of calcium), the contents of your vacuum cleaner bag, fruit waste (apple and pear cores, orange peel), and anything else that seems suitable. Do *not* add meat or fish scraps, as these can attract vermin. It is a good idea to have a 'scrap' bin in the kitchen intended for the compost heap as well as the usual rubbish bin.

I do recommend **compost activators** as they speed up the rotting-down process, and anything to achieve this is to be applauded. *Sulphate of ammonia*, sprinkled on every nine inch layer, is a good cheap source but of course proprietary brands of activators are available.

Ideally one should have two compost heaps—one that you are *using* and one that your are *making*.

I cannot leave this subject without recalling some years ago when hosting a 'Gardener's Question Time' in the Leeds area. A well-known gardener—who sadly, I believe, is now cultivating an allotment up above—suggested to a questioner that, when taking out runner bean and sweet pea trenches, he should place all his kitchen waste in the bottom of the open trenches and allow it to rot down in the fullness of time. This is *definitely wrong,* for as it rots down it will rob the soil of all its nitrogen. So do make your compost as suggested above, and, when it has reduced to a friable nature, barrow it to your trenches. (Compost activators have a high nitrogen content to replace the nitrogen used in the decomposition process.)

2. Farmyard Manure (from Stables, Crew Yards, etc.)

This is a prime source of humus, and readily available as we appear to have (at least in my neck of the woods) a rapidly expanding horse population and the said substance is not as scarce as it was a decade or so ago.

While animal manures are not particularly high in nutrients, they are of course totally organic and a rich source of humus. Ideally, the older the stack the better it is, fresh manure can present problems to young seedlings and roots. Lucky is the gardener who finds a pile of horse manure that is so old it resembles an odourless heap of peat. Do let me know the location if you do!

Do not be averse to using manure that contains a proportion of straw. Remember, this is an excellent means of flocculating heavy soils. Also it must be mentioned that bedding straw is extremely useful, as the urine contains more nutrient value than the 'solids'.

The only word of caution I would offer on stable manure is that in some stables there is a practice of bedding animals on sawdust or wood chippings. These, during the rotting-down process, can—like the fresh vegetative matter mentioned above—rob the manure of nitrogen and also encourage woodlice. So, if possible, avoid this type of manure.

3. Peat

We now come to a third source of humus—and quite a controversial one—peat. Peat is, of course, totally natural and 100% organic, but one must study one's own conscience on peat and the use thereof. I have considered this matter for many years and have my own personal views; suffice to say, I currently use peat-based composts as a growing medium, but do not use peat on my garden as a source of humus.

To summarise, garden compost will always be number one in my book as a prime source of humus because of its very nature and, of course, because it's free, which is never a bad thing! Number two on the list is farmyard manure, but it depends entirely on availability. Peat comes a very poor third, because of its high cost and because of the anti-peat lobby, which still waxes furiously in some parts.

pH

Incorporating some or all of the above, we have achieved a high humus level and the right soil structure. So what else do we need to consider before dashing out to sow and plant?

The answer is the **pH level** (potential of hydrogen), a measure of the acidity or alkalinity level of the soil. This may prove a little confusing at first, but once the basic principles have been grasped, pH problems will be simple to rectify.

The value for a neutral level is 7.0. Anything above this (7.1, 7.2, 7.3 and so on) is moving into the alkaline range; conversely, anything lower (6.9, 6.8, 6.7) is erring on the acid side. Generally, most plants function well in a soil reading of between 6.5 and 7.0—with a few notable exceptions. Heathers, rhododendrons, azaleas and other *ericaceous* (belonging to the 'heath' genus) plants all prefer an acid soil of between 5.5 and 6.0 and are described as 'acid-loving'. The important point is first to check your soil so that an adjustment can be made if necessary, and secondly to remember that, just as plants are living organisms and change during their various stages of growth, so our soil is ever-changing.

Adding manure, compost, peat and fertilisers has the effect of slowly lowering the pH; conversely acidic peaty soils can be raised by applying lime. Should a soil be too alkaline, the pH can be reduced by applying sulphur. It is important to check your soil every year or so, and of course to decide what you intend to grow—all part of garden planning. Very simple soil test kits are readily available from your nearest garden shop to measure either the pH alone or, with a more complete kit, to check both pH and the fertiliser

Azaleas and rhododendrons thrive in acid soil.

content. They vary in price, starting from a few pounds. I have checked the accuracy of these kits against laboratory reports, and can confirm that they are surprisingly precise. There are also several private laboratories around the country who can perform a specialist soil test service should you decide against the do-it-yourself method.

Whichever policy you pursue, may I again stress that an understanding of your soil, and of its changing condition is the key to success!

To conclude, I must warn you about the interaction between manure and lime. The two are not compatible, so the golden rule is that if lime is required, it should be applied as soon as the land is cleared and rough dug in the autumn; and any manure should not be spread until spring. Conversely, you can dress the garden with manure in the autumn and avoid applying lime until early spring. In a nutshell, try to allow approximately a six-month gap between the two dressings.

Geranium against a backdrop of lobelia.

Delphiniums, here producing massive spikes of blue flowers.‡

Fertilisers

The soil is a wonderful thing. Treat it like a good friend, give it the sort of nourishment it really appreciates, keep it in good heart, and it will reward you by growing almost everything your heart desires.

Fred Streeter

MUCH MYSTIQUE is attached to fertilisers, but if you really understand the basics, all becomes clear.

I often feel sorry for any new gardener who steps into a large, well-stocked garden centre for the first time to decide which fertiliser to buy. What a minefield! What a bewildering array of bottles, packets, drums and containers awaits you! Should you buy powder, granular, liquid, soluble powder? Or what about these fancy tablets or pins and spikes? And what if you inadvertently use a tomato feed on your lawn? Will the grass sprout baby tomatoes?

Let us begin by examining the requirements and uses of fertilisers. Stable manure and our garden compost contain surprisingly low levels of nutrients, and, as described in Chapter 1, their main function is to supply and build up the humus content to make the soil moisture-retentive and capable of making the best use of the nutrients we apply.

Whatever type of fertiliser we apply, it can only be absorbed by the plants' roots in a soluble form, so soil moisture content is essential to dissolve the solids. Most nutrients are absorbed by the roots, although a small proportion—particularly when the plant is under stress—can be taken up by the leaves (foliar feeding), but more of that later.

The three main nutrients essential to healthy plant growth are as follows.

Nitrogen (N) This is the element essential for healthy leaves and stems.
Phosphate (P) This promotes root growth.
Potash (K) This is the agent for plant ripening in all its forms, i.e. ripening of stems, intensifying colour in flowers, putting the colour and sweetness into fruits.

Based on this information, we can see that to grow a healthy plant with strong stems and leaves, a strong root structure to maintain these stems and leaves, and one that will achieve fruition in whatever form of fruit, flower or vegetable, a balance of the above-mentioned **N**, **P** and **K** is required. There are also various secondary elements needed — usually referred to as *trace elements* but more of that later. For now we will concentrate on the big three.

TYPES OF FERTILISER

Fertilisers can usually be divided into two basic categories—**solid** or **liquid**

Solids

Whether in powder or granular form, solid fertilisers are usually applied as a *base dressing* before planting, they are raked into the top few inches of our beds. A later top-up or a *top dressing* can often be beneficial during the season, either to supply a specific nutrient or as a pick-me-up for long-term crops, particularly after heavy rainfall when soils can become depleted.

Liquids

Liquid fertilisers have the advantage of being absorbed quickly, but the disadvantage of being short-term. They are, however, virtually a must for pot plants and the dedicated show grower.

We can also subdivide fertilisers into two other categories: **balanced**, and what are usually referred to as **straights**

Balanced

Balanced fertilisers contain a given ratio of N, P and K, which can vary depending on the type required. Base fertilisers are usually of the balanced variety, two typical examples being:

Growmore: (7% N; 7% P; 7% K). A chemical fully-balanced base fertiliser, the most widely used in the amateur range.
Fish, Blood and Bone: (usually 6% N; 6% P; 6% K). The organic alternative to Growmore, and fast gaining in popularity. It is much longer lasting but more expensive—you take your choice!

Straights

Straights contain just one of the three main nutrients, N, P or K, and are invaluable when a crop needs a boost of just one of these.

Finally, there is a third way of categorising fertilisers: organic or inorganic. This is rather an emotive and controversial subject.

Organic

As the name implies, organic fertilisers are derived from natural sources, e.g. fish blood and bone, bonemeal, fish meal, hoof horn, dried blood, etc. They have the advantage, being organic, of supplementing the humus level and are mostly slow-acting, thereby offering a longer period of nutrient release. The only real exception to this rule is dried blood, which is a quick-acting straight nitrogenous fertiliser.

Inorganic (Chemical)

These, unlike organic fertilisers, are mostly quick-acting but do nothing to improve your soil, either in humus content or texture. They are certainly cheaper than organic fertilisers and do have a part to play, unless you have definite views on only using natural materials—the choice must be yours.

Foliar Feeds

Foliar feeds are often referred to as a new technique and the greatest thing since sliced bread, but really the practice is as old as time itself.

It is true to say that if a plant is under stress, e.g. in drought conditions or with a waterlogged root ball, nutrients cannot be absorbed in the normal manner by the roots. Here foliar feeding comes into its own as leaves can and do absorb nutrients and can transfer them to the root mass. The rule for foliar feeding is to use any good liquid feed, mixed to half strength, and cover the leaf area to the run-off point (i.e. When the leaf surface is fully covered. Any that runs off is not needed).

NB: Do not apply foliar feeds in conditions of strong sunlight—particularly under glass—as scorching may occur.

A useful tip is to foliar feed plants immediately after planting. This gives the plants a flying start, as in the normal course of events the roots would need a little time to settle into their new environment and start taking up food.

Trace Elements

Trace elements are the micro-nutrients required in very small amounts but nonetheless essential in obtaining the best results from our plants. On fertiliser labels they are quantified in PPM (parts per million), and in some cases the amount is very low. The main trace elements are: *magnesium, manganese, molybdenum, zinc, copper, boron* and *iron*.

The good news is that your garden compost heap and stable manures are rich in trace elements, as are many of the commercial brands of fertilisers and liquid feeds, so generally the average garden soil is not deprived.

I think mention should be made here of the relationship between potash and magnesium. As described earlier, potash is the ripening agent—vital in producing ripe fruit and stems, inducing colour, building up a plant's resistance to disease and so on. However, without a supply of magnesium, the plant may not be able to use the potash, which remains 'locked up'. This is why tomato fertilisers and rose fertilisers have a high magnesium content.

EXAMPLES OF STRAIGHT FERTILISERS

Below are some of the most popular, easily-obtainable 'straight' fertilisers, with some useful notes as to their uses.

Bonemeal
Approximately 2% N; 25% P. Organic. A high source of phosphates; slow-acting. The coarser the grade, the slower the release.

Dried Blood
7%–14% N. Organic. A very useful, quick-acting 'booster'. Rather expensive.

Hoof and Horn
12%–14% N. A very slow-acting source of nitrogen. Organic.

Sulphate of Ammonia
21% N. Inorganic. A quick-acting nitrogen fertiliser. It tends to acidify soils and is widely used as an activator for garden compost. Do not mix with lime as this produces ammonia gas.

NB: As mentioned earlier, lime and fertiliser do not mix, and so should not be applied at the same time.

Sulphate of Potash
48% K. Inorganic. The most popular and widely-used source of potash.

Nitro-Chalk

15% N. Inorganic. A quick-acting nitrogenous 'boost'—useful in spring for a quick 'pick-me-up'. It is a chemical (and cheaper) alternative to dried blood.

Wood Ash

An organic source of K (potash). Its analysis varies widely between 5% and 10%, but it's worth remembering as it's a 'freebie'. It must be bagged and stored dry as soon as it's cool enough to handle—don't burn your fingers!

Epsom Salts

10% magnesium. Inorganic. A valuable source of magnesium, which is needed by, amongst others, tomatoes and roses, which have a high potash requirement. The potash can be 'locked up' without the presence of magnesium. It improves foliage on all plants and is one of the major trace elements.

 NB: Commercial Epsom salts, much cheaper than the type refined for human consumption, are available; seek them out.

Superphosphate

18% P. Inorganic. This is the most widely-used source of phosphate—the 'root maker'. It is slow-acting, but not easily leached from your soil.

Triple Superphosphate

48% P. A boosted-up version of Superphosphate. It is approximately three times as powerful.

There are many other 'straight' fertilisers, but the above are the most popular and easily obtainable.

IMPORTANT POINTS

1. The first essential is to ensure a high humus content, with the correct pH, before applying fertilisers.
2. The maxim should be 'little and often'. So many crops are ruined by excessive application of fertiliser.
3. Appreciate the benefits and advantages of both liquid and foliar feeding. They both give quick and visible short-term results.
4. Organics are longer lasting, but usually slower to act.

5. Understand the symbols N, P and K and how they relate to your crops' needs.

6. Remember that the seasons affect the needs of your plants. For example, in a hot sunny summer, more nitrogen is called for, whereas in a dull wet summer, we need to compensate by using more potash (K).

7. Finally, remember plant feeding is not, and never will be, an exact science, so common sense and experience are invaluable.

FERTILISER FORMULA

Some little time ago I prepared a fact sheet for BBC Radio Sheffield on how to produce various fertilisers on a DIY basis cheaply, and to take heed of various genera of plants and their needs. Obviously the cost is entirely dependent on the basic prices for the three active ingredients, but usually the larger quantity you buy, the cheaper the cost. I suggest you aim to use up stocks in a year, and store frost- and damp-free.

A good cheap general fertiliser can easily be made by buying the following three materials.

- Sulphate of ammonia: nitrogen for growth
- Superphosphate: for the roots
- Sulphate of potash: for ripening

They are best bought loose (although you can buy them pre-packed), and can be bought in pounds, kilos, stones or half-stones from your local garden shop, store or centre. Then *mix thoroughly* following the formula below (all parts by weight).

- 5 parts of sulphate of ammonia
- 6 parts of superphosphate
- 2 parts of sulphate of potash

Apply at two ounces per square yard and work it into the top 1–2 inches, preferably 7–10 days prior to planting in the spring. In existing borders and shrubberies apply evenly around plants, again two ounces per square yard, making sure that the formula doesn't come into contact with the foliage or growth. Apply in spring.

To help with the distribution of the fertiliser, and to save repeated weighing, carefully weigh out two ounces into a drinking cup and mark a line showing the height. Then just keep refilling up to the mark each time.

Other fertilisers for specific crops can be made with the same three ingredients, as follows (all parts by weight).

	Sulphate of ammonia	Superphosphate	Sulphate of potash
Brassicas/lettuce	2	3	1
Peas/beans	1	3	2
Root vegetables	1	4	2
Potatoes	3	4	2
Chrysanthemums	2	4	1

Again apply at two ounces per square yard.

Controlled Release Fertilisers

These I will discuss later under the heading 'Modern Science and Technology', but they need mentioning in this section on nutrients. This is another example of where we the amateurs can take advantage of a product originally developed for the commercial horticultural industry.

Controlled release fertilisers are an ingenious product. They are granular in form, each granule containing both N, P and K, and usually trace elements as well. They are held in a resin-coated matrix which breaks down as the temperature rises. Because plants require more nutrients as the temperature goes up, controlled release fertilisers make the nutrients available in harmony with the plants' needs. The speed of release can be adjusted by the degree of 'breakdown material' or of the porosity of the coating. These kinds of fertilisers can be formulated to provide, believe it or not, a release of nutrients over a period of eighteen months.

The advantage—particularly for container-grown subjects for the commercial grower—is obvious. Similarly, we the amateurs can use these with great success in hanging baskets, containers, window boxes, and so on, to make our feeding easier. There are also, of course, benefits in using these controlled release fertilisers in permanent beds such as roses and shrubs. I would recommend one that allows a 6–9 month release—one that needs replacing each spring would be ideal.

Fertilisers: A Summary

So what has the above taught us about the use and application of fertilisers? I often make the point that if someone could produce a fertiliser to fulfil the needs of all plants from asters to zinnias, for all seasons and all soil conditions, he would indeed be a wealthy person. But with a basic knowledge of the functions of N, P and K, a look at our plants and the weather, and a common-sense appreciation of the needs of the type of plant we are growing, a suitable feed can be given. All these variables are the reason behind the vast choice of fertilisers available; not, as has been suggested, because manufacturers try to blind us with science, nor that they are all the same, but put into different packages! Remember the professional farmer and grower uses more than one type and analysis, all governed by what he is growing and the season, and we on our own small scale should do the same.

Varied shapes and textures enhance any garden.‡

Garden Planning

God Almighty first planted a Garden; and indeed it is the purest of Human Pleasures

Sir Francis Bacon

IT IS SAID that pet owners, in time, often resemble their pets. The wisdom of this is frankly lost on me, but I do believe that a garden certainly reflects the personality of the gardener. Lucky is the person who takes over a new virgin plot and moulds it to his or her ideals; so many of us inherit someone else's dreams and ideas and at the end of the day never really have the garden of our desires.

As I write this I am reminded of a caller to one of my live phone-in broadcasts who told me that his daughter had just acquired a large, rather overgrown house and garden. What advice could I give? The most appropriate phrase that springs to mind is the old cliché 'Rome wasn't built in a day'.

My first task would be to take a piece of paper and make a scale drawing of the garden site: this is by far the easiest way of deciding what you have and haven't room for. I would most certainly test the soil for both pH and nutrient levels, and all plant debris and weeds should be cleared. Depending on the time of year, allow at least six months to ascertain what surprises—pleasant or otherwise—the garden contains. I'm referring particularly to bulbs and perennials that may be lying dormant awaiting the revival of spring before they burst forth.

One of the old ideas, often repeated, is the advice to a young couple confronted by a sea of mud on a newly-built housing estate: plant a privet hedge around the boundary; sow a lawn in the back garden; and in the front garden stick a dozen rose bushes—'this will give you a nice easy garden'. Frankly I can't think of anything more boring, but then gardens and gardening are very personal subjects. The number of people who have sought my advice on moving plants, shrubs and even tall trees goes to prove the importance of siting the 'permanent' plantings correctly in the first instance.

Different approaches to garden surfaces, walls and water features—a little thought and planning will give your garden individuality.

The front and back gardens are well known in many areas for what I call the 'lavatera explosion'. I'm not referring to the hardy type of annual mallow, such as the 'silver cup' variety, which is a superb species growing only approximately two feet high and which won many awards a decade or so ago, but the permanent bush type, which in three years can reach ten feet high, ten feet wide with three-inch-thick stems. These are fine if you have the area to contain them, but not really suitable for a pocket handkerchief plot!

For the inexperienced gardener starting completely afresh, I would strongly recommend the following guidelines:

1. Test the soil for pH level and nutrients. You can then adjust these by applying fertilisers and lime as required to provide the ideal growing conditions for your choice of plants.

2. Have a 'board meeting' with other members of the household involved with the garden, to decide what you wish to grow and how much time can be devoted to its upkeep.

3. Make a scale drawing of your various ideas so that a plan—maybe fairly long term—can be formulated.

4. As a first priority, lay down permanent or semi-permanent paths of concrete, paving blocks, or slabs. It is so much easier when working from a dry and level base.

5. Remember that curved or irregular-shaped beds give a garden character, and curved paths create the illusion of greater size.

6. Avoid 'flat' planting. Instead, use occasional 'dot' plants such as columnar specimens, *acer brilliantisimum*, grafted as a standard, or *prunus amanogowa*, again slender and upright and acting as a focal point. Height and contrast lend so much character to a garden.

7. If you've just moved into a new area, have a look round to see—if possible over a full season—what grows well and appeals to you. With the best will in the world, catalogues and books tend to 'guild the lily', and what does well in Devon may struggle to survive in the Pennines. Take advantage of local garden clubs and societies; most allotment societies will welcome you as a private garden member, and by paying the annual peppercorn membership fee you can buy many of your sundries and requirements at very reduced prices, as well as getting invaluable free advice from other members.

Gardeners are always willing to pass on advice. Consult your local library for specialist books and don't forget the gardening press.

8. Don't underestimate the role of features in forming a garden's character. Typical examples are: arches, gazebos, tubs, urns, hanging baskets, unusual plant containers and, perhaps the most tranquil feature of all, moving or running water. Nothing is more peaceful or restful, offering so much scope and beauty.

9. Try to create colour and interest all the year round by judicious selective planting. Remember your garden is on view fifty-two weeks a year.

10. Make haste slowly: a garden should be a work of love. If you do wish to adopt a mercenary attitude, a well-kept garden will indeed enhance the appearance of your property when it comes to selling it. But, after all that time and effort, could you bear to part with it? On that note I leave this chapter with the following quotation:

The garden that is finished is dead.

H.E. Bates

A splash of colour brightens the border in late spring.

All-Year Gardening

*It is a blessed sort of work, and if Eve had had a spade in
Paradise and known what to do with it we should not have
had all that sad business of the apple.*

Countess Von Arnim,
Elizabeth and her German Garden (1898)

ALTHOUGH we are very much at the mercy of Nature and the
changing seasons, judicious use of various basic equipment means that
all-year gardening is possible. A greenhouse, for example, is like an
extra arm to the keen gardener, and what is a greenhouse without a
cold-frame or cloches? England is a treasure chest of stately homes and
walled kitchen gardens, all featuring greenhouses with adjacent cold-
frames. The Victorian gardeners knew what it was all about! In this
respect, we also owe a debt to the plant raisers and seed producers
whose expertise can now give us a much-extended season. For
instance, we can now enjoy lettuce virtually 365 days of the year by
choosing the right varieties and making full use of frames and cloches.
When I look back at my old gardening diaries of just a few years ago,
I'm amazed by the fact that I no longer grow 90% of the varieties I
grew then: quite simply they've been superseded by better strains.

THE GARDEN DIARY

This incidental remark brings me very nicely to a most important
piece of equipment for any gardener: a diary or growing plan. It is so
important to be able to know exactly what we planted when and
where and the results obtained. I personally use a simple flat spiral-
bound notebook with lined pages. A simple plan — say for bedding
plants — could be set out as follows:

BEDDING PLANTS

Seed supplier	Variety name	Method and date of sowing	Results

This means one can always refer to previous years and repeat successes or avoid repeating failures. The method that suits me and my growing is to use one page for each category: one for veg, one for early chrysanths, late chrysanths, dahlias, gladioli, sweet peas, and so on. Obviously, you can alter the headings to suit you and your crops. (A brief note here: for chrysanths, the stopping and flowering dates are crucial if you join the fraternity of show growers.

From a practical point of view, a garden diary means you can avoid using labels, which, apart from the cost, are so easily lost and often quickly become illegible. If you grow any plants in rows, i.e. chrysanths, gladioli, dahlias or sweet peas, it is extremely easy to draw up a plan each year for these so that it becomes a simple task to locate each variety and carry out any culture they require.

Flowers, foliage, attractive stems and barks are all easily produced outdoors—even in the frozen north—but add a greenhouse and cold-frame and a whole new gamut is opened up for us. If you go one step further with a heated greenhouse, the world is indeed your oyster.

The seeds people have really done us proud, and continue to do so, with better and higher-yielding strains of vegetables. Frankly the mind boggles when one compares the crops we readily achieve today to those of only a few years ago. This is all the more reason to keep records and be prepared to experiment with new strains and varieties.

The preparatory work out of the way, we can move on to the next part and the real 'nitty gritty': What Do We Grow?

Daffodils, resplendent against the spring sky.

Fruit

What beautiful fruit! I love fruit when it's expensive.
Sir Arthur Wing Pinero
(from The Second Mrs Tanqueray, Act I)

THE BRITISH ISLES are fortunate still to possess so many examples of the old walled fruit gardens with their fan-shaped plum, peach, cherry and other mouth-watering fruit trees, some encapsulated in massive fruit cages and structures. These were always a source of wonder to me in my formative years in horticulture.

Today—and here again we must pause to doff our caps to the scientists and plant breeders—fruit growing for the amateur has entered a new dimension. New techniques and varieties now make fruit growing not just a possibility but a definite must for even the smallest garden; in fact you don't even need a garden to enjoy the thrill and taste of producing your own fresh fruit.

I. Soft/Cane Fruits

These deserve a place in everyone's garden and are the first priority in the world of fruit growing. This is because they occupy a small space in relation to the crops they produce and, from a purely financial aspect, they really do give value for money (although we're not gardening for profit, of course!).

RASPBERRIES

A row of these should be found in every garden. They grow upwards on stiff canes and therefore don't take up a large area and they are the easiest crop to gather, the fruit growing invariably between waist and head height with no vicious thorns.

Soil and Siting

The important point is correct preparation of the site, which means thorough digging, removing all weeds and debris. Leave three weeks and then repeat the same treatment. The reason for this is that raspberries are shallow-rooted and after planting should not be hoed, but hand-weeded or treated with glyphosate on any soft weed growth. Without a doubt the correct and easiest way to grow these fine berries is in a single or double row, preferably running west to east, and they will perform quite well in a semi-shady spot. Strong supports should be put in every 10–12 feet, with horizontal straining wires, ideally one approximately four feet high and another at six feet. Plastic-covered wire is preferable to tie the canes to, as it is long lasting. The best planting time is October or November, so curb your impetuosity! New canes when bought are already pruned back, so it will take two years before they bear fruit; after that you can expect a real harvest every year. (This applies to the ever-popular summer-fruiting variety; more about the autumn-fruiting variety later.) Canes should be planted 18–20 inches apart and a good general fertiliser should be raked into the top 2–3 inches at approximately four ounces per square yard. You'll note that force of habit means that I still work in imperial measurements—I trust that readers will be able to follow me.

Like all cane fruit, raspberries respond very well to mulching and the use of potash. With this in mind, a dressing in late autumn of sulphate of potash, two ounces per yard, or bonfire ash (*must be fresh*), followed by a further similar application in March should give super yields.

Pruning

Summer raspberries are simplicity itself. During a growing season, both fruit on existing canes and new canes for next year are produced. After fruiting, all the old canes that have carried the crop are cut back to 2–3 inches above ground level; these are easily distinguished by their dark brown colour. The new canes—next year's crop—are a light green colour, and should be tied in to the horizontal straining wires, not more than five per plant. A very good tip that is not widely stated is to snip the top of all canes in late February, just removing the top inch or so. This induces and speeds up the formation of fruiting laterals.

Pests and Diseases

Aphids should be avoided at all costs as these transmit the dreaded virus diseases. Prevention being better than cure, a regular spraying routine with a systemic aphicide every twenty-one days is recommended; this can be applied as a three-ingredient 'cocktail' using an aphicide, fungicide and a foliar feed. This should ensure a super crop.

Succulent raspberries—
the queen of summer fruit.‡

Plump gooseberries
just right for eating.‡

NB: Do not spray when in flower. Stop when flowers start to form and do not begin again until the fruit is set.

Raspberry Beetle (Fruit Maggot). Guard against this by spraying at the *pink fruit stage* with Malathion or similar. One spraying is usually sufficient.

Varieties
Malling Delight. An early/mid-season variety, aphid-resistant with large fruit.
Glen Prosen. A heavy cropper with a good taste.
Malling Jewel. An old variety, tried and tested, with a super taste.
Autumn-Fruiting Types. If raspberries are your thing, no lover of same should be without at least a short row of autumn-fruiting plants. These produce less vigorous canes due to the fact that, unlike summer-fruiting varieties, they produce both canes and fruit in one season. Fruiting time is September to November and pruning consists of cutting all canes down to ground level in January. The new growth is much shorter than its summer-fruiting cousins and hardly needs a supporting wire. All feeding and other instructions are as for the summer varieties, but the main advantage of growing both types is that the joy of raspberries can be experienced from early July through to October. What a prospect! The autumn raspberry to choose is *Autumn Bliss*, a new variety that stands out head and shoulders over its rivals.

GOOSEBERRIES

Gooseberries are probably the Cinderella of soft fruit and unjustly maligned by many. The older varieties certainly suffer greatly from the unsightly and debilitating American mildew, and the gooseberry saw-fly caterpillar is certainly capable of stripping all foliage in a matter of days—it has quite an appetite! However, gooseberry bushes are nonetheless an efficient high-yielding factory of soft fruit, and well worth growing—particularly if a few selected varieties of both culinary and dessert varieties can be accommodated.

Pruning
Approximately one-third of all branches should be removed each winter and the weakest of any crossing branches should be cut out completely. Try to maintain an open centre in each bush: good air circulation helps to minimise American mildew. When buying bushes, a short sturdy main stem is ideal, and the bush should have a goblet shape.

Varieties

a) Culinary

Greenfinch. This is reputed to be mildew-resistant—a real bonus.

Careless. An old variety, a heavy cropper that can be susceptible to mildew, so spray early to avoid it.

Leveller. A dual-purpose plant. Pick early for use in pies, or leave to develop for dessert.

b) Dessert

Leveller. Produces heavy crops with a good flavour—tried and tested.

Whinham's Industry. This one has stood the test of time. Attractive large red berries, but slow to mature.

Planting and Feeding

Planting and feeding are very much the same as for raspberries, potash again being the main requirement. However, an excess of potash can 'lock up' your soil's magnesium so a spray of commercial Epsom salts (dilute four ounces to one gallon of water) would be a good practice every two years in late spring. Alternatively, commercial Epsom salts can be applied dry at one ounce per square yard in March.

Cultivation

Here again deep hoeing should be avoided, and surface weeds can be dealt with by our friend glyphosate. *Caution:* spray only the weeds.

BLACKCURRANTS

All dieticians extol the beneficial properties of Vitamin C, of which blackcurrants are an excellent source. And what a joy they would be if only the dreaded *'big bud'* could be eliminated—more of which later.

Planting

The site for blackcurrants should be considered carefully, as the main requirement is shelter from cold winds; a windbreak can be a great help. An open sunny spot is desirable, but a sheltered site is vital for adequate pollination, the reason being that flowers appear very early and consequently bees and other pollinating insects must be encouraged to visit. October and November are the best planting months.

Feeding

Blackcurrants are greedy plants, so a heavy dressing of manure or compost at planting can only be very beneficial. Subsequent applications of 1½ ounces per square yard of sulphate of potash each October followed by a general fertiliser at the same rate each February will be of great help in generating bumper crops.

Pruning

After planting, cut down all branches to within 1–2 inches of ground level. This sounds drastic, and it also means that you have no harvest in the first year, but after that it's all joy. In the following autumn, cut out any weak shoots to ground level. Each autumn after that, cut out just the oldest shoots after fruiting, as these will be replaced by new shoots *ad infinitum*.

Mulching

Like all soft fruit, a 2–3-inch deep mulch each autumn performs three vital functions.

1. It keeps roots warm.
2. It stifles weeds.
3. It conserves moisture (and blackcurrants are real boozers!)

Pests and Diseases

Be alert to *aphids*, which spread diseases. The *red spider mite* can also be extremely debilitating, so take steps to eradicate them, as prevention is better than cure. Now the dreaded *big bud*, which is easy to recognise—as the name implies, a distinct swelling of the buds appears—but very difficult to cure. Affected buds can be removed and burnt. If the disease persists, the bush should be removed and burnt.

Reversion (often called 'nettle leaf') is also fairly common. The leaves become ferny and much smaller, and again I'm afraid there is no real cure, so remove bushes and burn them. You should always have a clean culture, free of aphids, which are the disease carriers, and buy 'certified' stock from a reputable source. I always feel that, with all types of fruit, specialist sources are by far the best.

Varieties

Ben Connan. I strongly recommend this new variety. It is an early cropper, with high yield and a high standard of disease resistance, but its main claim to fame is the size of the berries: over half an inch in diameter, so picking is made easy.

Wellington XXX. An old but reliable variety that yields well, but may be superseded in popularity by *Ben Connan*.

Ben Alder. This is a late variety and thus extends the fruiting season of blackcurrants. Because it flowers late, it usually avoids spring frost damage.

Hybrid Berries. Here again the plant hybridisers have given us some very interesting soft cane fruits such as Tayberry, Boysenberry, and so on. They are always worth experimenting with if soft fruit is your thing. Fruit from these hybrids is rarely available in the shops.

BLACKBERRIES

Here again vast strides have been made by our plant scientists, and the new cultivated strains are a far cry from the blackberries of the hedgerows. Many of the new varieties, though not all, are thornless. I can still remember the lacerations when, as a youth, I went blackberrying in short trousers and sleeveless shirt! Also, of course, the flavour is much improved and today's yields are outstanding.

Planting and Siting
Blackberries relish a good feed, so prepare the site thoroughly and incorporate a good supply of stable manure or compost, enriching it even further with a dusting of general fertiliser: fish blood and bone being ideal. Blackberries are particularly suited for training against a wall or fence and will succeed in shade, and even against a north-facing wall.

Pruning
Pruning couldn't be easier: simply cut down all fruiting branches to ground level immediately after cropping.

Varieties

a) Thornless
It should be pointed out that the thornless varieties are always less vigorous than the thorny types.

Waldo. This is a new variety from the United States, and has arrived with a big reputation. It is compact, so well suited for the small garden.

Loch Ness. Another new variety, this time from north of the Border; again, this one is a compact grower.

Almost too good to eat!‡

Oregon Thornless. This is the forerunner of the thornless varieties. It is rather late to crop, but has a fine taste.

b) Thorny

Bedford Giant. An early variety. A vigorous grower producing high yields of quality fruit.

Ashton Cross. Probably one of the best-tasting of all varieties, but mind the thorns!

Himalayan Giant. A native of western Europe, despite the name! It produces great crops, but the thorns are vicious! The taste is rather sharp, but refreshing.

STRAWBERRIES

I suppose strawberries in our culture will always be associated with images of sunshine, cream and Wimbledon. They have a relatively short season, but remain extremely popular.

Planting

Ideally, strawberries should be grown in a three-year cycle, so when planning (back to the notebook!), a bed should be marked out allowing sufficient width for three rows. The new plants should be planted down the middle and the left-hand side should be planted with next year's plants; likewise the right-hand side accommodates the following year's plants. These should be labelled, naturally, '1', '2', and '3'. By the fourth year Row 2 is completely replaced and so on *ad infinitum*, so that all rows are either one, two or three years old.

Weeds, birds and slugs are the main problems for strawberries, so good preparation in the first instance is of paramount importance. Clean, well-dug land, that is high in humus and water-retentive is vital. A sunny open aspect is required, and try to avoid hollows or frost pockets when choosing your site. New plants from a reputable source should be your first choice: virus-resistant certified stock is always available if you want it. Planting should be carried out in September or October, planting eighteen inches apart in rows. Guard against slugs, and, after fruit-set, cloches or nets will ensure you and not the birds enjoy the results.

Runners

The summer after planting will yield a moderate crop, and also a supply of runners, which will provide your second-year plants. Each runner—which resembles brown string with tiny plantlets every six inches or so—should be pegged down and will readily form roots at each tuft of growth or plantlet. No more than two plants should be rooted from each runner: the ones nearest the mother plant are the strongest, so cut off the runners after the second plantlet, and also any surplus runners, so that the plant's energy is not wasted.

The plantlets root readily if pegged down with a piece of wire, but a more tidy and successful method is to fill three-inch pots with a suitable compost (soilless, or John Innes No. 1) and sink these in the ground below the plantlets you intend to use. Peg them down with wire and within a month you'll be able to sever the runners and dig out the pots, each now containing a well-rooted young strawberry plant. This method means that the area for your second row is left unobstructed while you weed and prepare the ground. Ensure that the new row is planted by the end of October.

Early Fruit

Greenhouse owners can enjoy really early crops by selecting some of the better and strongest young plantlets and, after following the above method, transfer the plantlets into five-inch pots with John Innes No. 2 compost. Over-winter these in a frost-free greenhouse keeping them just moist, and place them on a high shelf to give them as much light as possible. Remove any decaying leaves and in March give them a weak concentration of high-potash liquid feed (your tomato feed at half-strength would be ideal). As warmth and light increases, give more water and feed. Flowers should form in mid-April and you can aid pollination by lightly using a camel hair paintbrush to transfer the pollen. With only average luck, you should be enjoying fruit by mid-May. Don't expect a huge crop, but at least you'll get an early taste of summer!

Varieties

Elsanta. A fairly new variety that is proving very popular both commercially and with the amateur. A high yield and a good taste.

Hapil. This one makes picking easy with huge fruit with good colour and taste. Early season.

EM 227. This one's so new it's only got a number! An early-season variety with a strong pedigree that has received warm reviews.

Cambridge Favourite. An oldie, but the one all newer varieties are judged by.

Honeyoye. A strange name, but the earliest-fruiting variety—a new one that is proving very popular. It has a super taste and large berries.

Pests and Diseases

As mentioned, birds and slugs are hindrances to strawberry growers. Both can be controlled, but vigilance is important as well as good garden hygiene, i.e. take care to remove all weeds and debris.

Red Spider Mite. These are a real threat and should be guarded against. Hardly visible to the naked eye, they turn the foliage a coppery colour and have a seriously debilitating effect on the plants and, of course, reduce crops drastically. Good regular spraying on a routine basis is advised—as usual prevention is better than cure.

II. Top Fruit

APPLES

When thinking of England and home-grown fruit, the mind immediately conjures up visions of *Cox's, Laxton's* and *James Grieve*—real English apples that have stood the test of time. We now have a national apple day, and, in my book, rightly so. Modern science and technology (I have returned to my favourite hobby horse) has given us dwarfing root-stocks and strains which mean that top fruit can be grown in a confined space. In fact, a garden is not required at all: by using large pots and containers a paved area can still produce superb top fruit, and you don't need a ladder to harvest it! There is, however, a price to pay for growing apples on these new dwarf root-stocks: we must accept that yields will naturally be much lower than on a conventional tree and certain requirements regarding staking, pruning and feeding must be observed.

Before discussing varieties of actual fruit, it is a good idea to decide on the root-stocks available and which suit what site and position.

Root Stocks

M27. This is the dwarfest of all, giving a fruiting mature tree of approximately six feet in height. It can be grown as a 'super column' (i.e. a single main stem with short stubby laterals or branches pruned to 6–9 inches) or as a mini bush. They crop early in life, give large-size apples, and a good specimen will yield thirty-plus. They can be grown in either beds or large pots, being particularly suitable for pot culture. The basic needs are as follows:

1. Start with a twelve-inch diameter pot, preferably terracotta, as a thin-walled plastic pot carries the risk of frost penetration in a hard winter and hence a risk of root damage.

Apple—Ellison's Orange Pippin.‡

2. Transfer to a 15–16-inch pot after two years. Don't use anything bigger.

3. Use John Innes No. 3 compost. Soilless composts do not have either the life or the bulk to do the tree justice.

4. A short sturdy stake is necessary throughout the tree's life, as the very nature of these dwarf stocks means they don't have the root vigour required to be self-supporting. Certain catalogues may say otherwise, but I do recommend using a support.

5. Feed regularly (foliar feeding is a great tonic occasionally) and never let the plant go short of water. This is vital for, if the roots dry out, at best the crop will be nil and at worst the tree will die. Don't say you've not been warned!

The advantages of pot-grown mini-fruit are tremendous. Apart from making fruit growing a possibility for homes without gardens, it also means great flexibility. For example, most varieties require two different plants for pollination to occur, so at blossom time the two pots can be placed close together in a sheltered spot. Similarly, in a really severe winter pots can be lifted into a greenhouse or conservatory for a few days to miss the worst of the weather. However, a note of caution here: don't mollycoddle apple trees, you'll do more harm than good. The secret is simply to ensure that the roots do not freeze solid. Bubble plastic wrapped around the pot is a great help, and a three-inch mulch of straw on the surface will do nothing but good. Of course, an important advantage of pot growing is that you can place the pots wherever you think they look best.

M9. This is the next size up in root-stocks. It still produces mini-trees, though these have a slightly more robust root formation, and a mature tree grows to approximately eight feet in height. This is the tallest type that we can accommodate in a container; anything taller than this must be a free-standing garden tree in either of the following root-stocks.

M26. Intended for the medium-sized garden, and it produces excellent root formation. It is free-standing and has a mature height of 10–12 feet.

MM106. For the large garden as it will finish at a height of 12–18 feet; it is not suitable for tiny courtyard gardens.

Varieties

Choice of apple variety is very much a matter of personal preference, both in dessert and cooking apples. We are spoiled in the UK by the vast range available to us, so care should be taken in choosing. 'Family' trees are available from specialist sources, which are grafted with two or even three varieties, meaning very good pollination and of course the delights of sampling two or three apples from one tree—what a prospect! I must add a word of caution on family trees: over the years the strongest-growing variety may overwhelm the weaker-growing strains and so make the tree 'out of balance'.

Pruning

This often frightens the new gardener more than any other task in fruit growing. For apples, no pruning should be required in the first year; your supplier should have done all that is necessary. Fruiting does not take place till the second and subsequent years.

Golden Rule. Winter pruning promotes growth; summer pruning restricts vigour but encourages fruit formation. Fruit buds require maximum light and sun to form fruit so an open framework is desirable. An old country saying, that I often repeat when asked about pruning apple trees, is that a pigeon should be able to fly through it without touching any branch. Obviously, all dead wood should be removed on existing old trees and any crossing branches should be avoided; summer pruning back to fruiting spurs is a must. On the other hand, over-vigorous pruning in winter can have disastrous consequences, but a compromise must be achieved.

Feeding

The future of the tree and therefore the yield is determined by three factors: the root-stock chosen; the variety chosen; and the planting. Prepare the site very carefully by digging thoroughly, removing all weeds and stones, and incorporating lots of life-giving humus. Apply a good dressing of fertiliser and *plant very firmly*. In the first year water, water and water again. This is the time when you set the foundation for the rest of the tree's life. If planted in grass it's far better to remove a three-foot circle of grass round the new tree, so that its roots are not competing for nutrients in the first year or two. Once the tree is mature, this ceases to be a problem.

Pests and Diseases

Many books have been written on this subject, but the following should enable you to maintain a healthy tree. Once again, prevention will always be better than cure.

Winter tar-washing is a great way of removing lots of unwanted guests lying dormant during winter ready to pounce in spring. Grease-banding should become a regular routine task, and a codling moth trap set in the tree at the end of May can work wonders. Make sure the tree is well supplied with magnesium, as this promotes quality fruit: a dusting of Epsom salts in March is indicated here, or, easier still, add it to your spring fertiliser dressing at one ounce per square yard. Finally, *Dithane 945* is an essential fungicide for top fruit.

All the above may seem hard work—and expensive—but once you sink your teeth into a ripe English apple, it's more than worthwhile.

PEARS

In our region (north of England), pears need a sheltered site and more warmth than apples. In most cases they need a pollinator, though Conference is the exception to the rule and can produce quite a decent crop on its own. The root-stocks widely available are Quince 'A' or 'C', the latter being by far the most dwarf, and designed for the small garden. The taste and texture of a ripe juicy pear beggars description and over the years Conference and Comice—or, to give it its full title, *Doyenne Du Comice*—have held sway with the English palate. I do, however, recommend the less famous variety bred from the aforementioned pair known as **Concorde**, which is a heavy cropper and should be pollinated with either Conference or Williams. Concorde, when grafted on Quince 'C', produces a dwarf compact tree of approximately seven feet in height. Aim for a soil pH of approximately 6–7.

PLUMS

Again, another tree not immediately suited to the smaller garden and the frozen north! It must be stressed that plums flower early, so the site needs to be chosen carefully: frost pockets must be avoided at all costs. A south- or west-facing aspect with a moisture-retentive soil of near neutral pH is perfect.

Root-stocks

Credit is again due to the backroom boys for developing a superb new dwarfing root-stock, named 'Pixy'. Made for the small garden, it will become a mature tree of 8–9 feet in height, and they should be planted approximately eight feet apart.

*A well-known favourite—
Conference pear.*‡

*Victoria plum—crops
in early September.*‡

Pollination
The good news regarding plums is that many of the best varieties are self-fertilising so only one tree is necessary, if space is at a premium.

Varieties
The choice is wide and mouth-watering but below are a few ideas (all of them self-fertilising).

a) Dessert
Sancustus Hubertus. Probably the earliest of all plums, fruiting in July in northern England.
Victoria. The best known of all; crops in early September.
Valor. This is a new one that crops in late September to follow *Victoria.* It has a good taste and heavy crop.

b) Culinary
Czar. An old tried-and-tested variety for pies and jams. An early-to-mid August cropper, very dark and exotic.
Marjorie's Seedling. The last to fruit and a very reliable cooker. It crops in early October.

In conclusion on fruit, I must emphasise that the varieties discussed are my own personal preferences. However, where root-stocks are concerned, it is vital that you are supplied with the correct one for the purpose intended.

An early flowering chrysanthemum—Bill Else.‡

Flowers

I have a garden of my own,
Shining with flowers of every hue,
I loved it dearly while alone,
But I shall love it more with you.
                                   Thomas Moore, 1835

THE JOY OF A GARDEN is predominantly a visual one, and we
have it within our power to create an impressive spectacle with the
vast choice and variety of flowers that grow so well in these islands
of ours. From the stately home to the humble cottage garden, there
is a long tradition of flower growing in Britain. In doing so, we are
preserving our heritage while at the same time creating a joy to
behold.

Digressing completely for a moment, I am reminded of the story
of a new curate in a remote West Riding parish out for a walk
around his new village on his first week there. He came across a
superb cottage, the garden resplendent with flowers, the vegetable
patch containing rows of immaculate produce in orderly lines, not a
weed in sight. In the middle of the garden was old Amos, well into
his seventies, pulling his hoe through imaginary weeds. The curate
called out: 'Morning my man. What a lovely garden. I'm the new
curate at your church.' Old Amos paused, looked up and said, 'Aye, I
guessed you were'. 'Yes,' replied the curate, 'It's amazing what God
and man can achieve in a garden.' 'Yes, I'm sure ye be reight, Vicar,'
said Amos, 'But it were a reight ruddy mess when he had it on his
own'.

CHRYSANTHEMUMS

In my early days on allotments, the flowers that first attracted me—
and I'm still as keen on them today—were chrysanthemums. I began
cultivating these flowers way back when and have enjoyed a
constant romance with them ever since, and I'm sure my love for
them will continue. I recently gave a series of talks entitled 'Why
Chrysanthemums?', and a condensed version of the lectures follows

below. I hope it helps me win over a few new converts to the flower that is rightly described as the 'Queen of the Autumn'.

No other family of flowers can offer such a wide range of colour and form, the ability to bloom from August to Christmas without resorting to special manipulation, and such long vase life as a cut flower. Admittedly, after October a greenhouse is needed to protect the late blooms, but with no more than a small growing patch and an 8' x 6' greenhouse, a succession of long-lasting blooms is readily yours. The chrysanthemum is a most accommodating plant, ideally suited to our climate. All it asks is a light position, to be kept staked and watered, reasonably weed-free and fed, and for this it will reward you handsomely. Being a surface-rooting plant, plenty of humus and/or a mulch is extremely beneficial, and a regular spraying routine is certainly advisable. See below for more detail on this.

The selection of variety is a very personal matter, as always, and the choice can frankly be bewildering. Put simply, chrysanthemums fall into two main categories: spray and bloom. 'Spray' are the multi-headed flowers in a glorious range of colours in daisy-type, double, anemone-centred, and so on; 'bloom' are the large stately blooms in incurved, reflexed, decorative or single form.

They can also be categorised according to growing season. 'Earlies' are planted out in the garden and flower *in situ* around September; 'lates' are usually grown in pots and left to stand outside all summer, then are lifted into the protection of a greenhouse around early October, flowering in November and December. Thus by growing both types, we can enjoy continuous blooms over approximately five months—a real reward for our efforts. I strongly urge all interested readers to join the National Chrysanthemum Society and/or a local branch. Your circle of friends and knowledge of chrysanthemums will increase enormously! A word of caution is in order: once smitten by the chrysanthemum-growing bug, there is virtually no cure!

General Culture

All chrysanthemums are vegetatively propagated (grown from cuttings), which are rooted very early in the year. They should be planted out around mid-May and are usually grown in rows with a strong support at each end and a horizontal straining wire. Each plant needs its own stout cane and these are tied to the horizontal wire: 15–18 inches between plants is ideal. A rich soil and a mulch in late June works wonders both in conserving moisture and in preventing weeds. As chrysanths are surface-rooting, this is one crop on which the hoe should not be used. Try to keep the plants well tied and free of weeds and pests.

Stopping

'Stopping' is the removal of the growing tip to ensure that the plant produces several arms, each of which will bear flowers. Timing is of paramount importance to the show-growers, but, as a general rule of thumb, stopping around mid-June will yield excellent results in September. Four or five stems per plant is ideal for a profusion of good, long-lasting flowers *par excellence*.

When buds appear—usually in late July—the *bloom* type should have all side-buds and shoots removed, leaving just one central crown bud on each stem. With *sprays*, the large central bud is removed to produce a balanced multi-bloom head.

Pests and Diseases

Chrysanthemums are so rewarding that I suppose we must expect problems. After all, if it was so easy, the challenge would be lost.

Aphids. These should not be too much of a problem. However, greenfly will infest your plants unless you take effective measures to control them. Organic sprays are available.

Leaf Miner. These can make the leaves unsightly with their tunnelling activities; again take action against them with your trusty spray.

Capsid Bug. A pernicious visitor, so here again take action.

Western Flower Thrip. A relatively new 'baddie' that has come to try us—but can be overcome.

Black Cotton or Black Melon Aphid (Aphis Gossypii). This is the latest scourge of the chrysanth-grower. Briefly, it has appeared in the last year or two, being an import from warmer climes, as the name suggests. Nicotine is a certain controller, which is good news; however, nicotine is banned to the amateur under the 1986 pesticide regulations! Nonetheless, if we are ever-vigilant, and if we use yellow sticky traps in our greenhouses and as wide a range of aphicides as is available to us—including a mixture of paraffin and soft soap—I am sure we will win through. Do ensure all bought-in plants are clean on arrival. No doubt the scientists will come up with a cure before too long—I wish them well.

White Rust and Mildew. These are the two main diseases to afflict chrysanthemums, but a good systemic fungicide used on a regular basis will control them.

I will close this short section on my beloved chrysanths by reaffirming that all the effort spent growing them has proved worthwhile—I don't regret a minute of the time. Although I sound

Mixed dahlias provide a stunning floral display.‡

very enthusiastic with the pesticides, I must point out that I do not spray indiscriminately; however I strongly believe that prevention is better than cure, so for me judicious spraying is a must.

DAHLIAS

Dahlias are possibly the most colourful and rewarding flowers for any garden—and so accommodating. Like chrysanths, they offer a riot of form and colour: from the exquisite tiny pom dahlias to the large cacti and decorative varieties. I always refer to dahlias as true 'cut and come again' flowers. Admittedly, their vase life is short, but this is no problem when fresh blooms appear with such speed and regularity.

Dahlias are frost-tender, so wait until the end of May or early June before planting them out. The first autumnal frosts will blacken them, so a fast growth pattern is essential, and they thrive on a high moisture content, so keep them well-watered, mulched and dead-headed. At the end of the season all plants will have produced tubers, and these should be carefully lifted and dried, dusted with flowers of sulphur and stored frost-free for the following season.

There are several possibilities when propagating the following year. The tubers (check they are firm and plump) can be directly planted in early May. Alternatively, with greenhouse facilities, tubers can be started into growth at the end of March and new cuttings rooted as they form; or, as tubers sprout, they can be cut into sections, each with a new growth evident and planted out in late May. Cuttings (or 'green' plants) are the way for better plants and present a lower risk of transmitting virus diseases.

There are countless varieties of dahlia; if you visit a couple of the larger shows you will find the choice bewildering. A point to remember is that varieties that keep winning must have something special. I will expand on this subject in the 'Growing for Showing' section.

Site and Cultivation

Dahlias thrive in an open sunny spot. Give them plenty of water and in the early stages feed them with plenty of nitrogen to encourage fast growth. Switch to a high-potash feed when the flower buds form. Mulch well to conserve moisture.

Pests and Diseases

Everyone talks of *earwigs* on dahlias; if you are aware of the problem, it should be easy to counteract it. Several chemicals provide good control of earwigs, namely Permethrin and Pirimiphos

(Methyl), which are both widely available. Also, a small plant pot filled with straw and suspended upside down on the supporting canes makes a simple but effective trap—remove it daily and dispose of all you trap. The show-growers also lightly smear a band of Vaseline round the choice bloom stems, which prevents earwigs reaching the show blooms. Slugs can be a problem on young plants, so take precautions. Similarly, spray against aphids which are the carriers of the dreaded virus diseases.

The main disease of dahlias is commonly referred to as **Stunt Virus**. This is a very nasty problem where a young plant becomes knarled, arthritic, twisted and stunted in growth—hence its name. The condition is easily recognisable, and the affected plant often tries to throw up a twisted mutation of a flower. There is no cure, so the plant must be dug up and burnt, cleansing the site with a strong application of either Jeyes Fluid or Armillatox.

SWEET PEAS

I feel that, to follow dahlias, we should discuss sweet peas. Although they are not at all similar in other ways, the sweet pea is another 'cut and come again' flower. Graceful, rich in perfume and delicate in form, it is a true aristocrat and a perfect English flower. It is easy to grow, but to produce the eighteen-inch long stems with five flowers, perfectly placed on each stem, does require a little more skill than luck.

The better plants (and, of course, blooms) are produced from autumn-sown seeds (October and November) over-wintered in a cold frame or greenhouse. Plants should be grown very cool, and, as the pea produces a long tap-root, special sweet pea tubes of cardboard or whalehide are ideal, as they biodegrade totally, thus avoiding root disturbance when planted out. After germination the plant should be 'stopped' or pinched after the second pair of leaves; this encourages a further lateral to be produced from the junction of the main stem and the first pair of leaves. The reason for this is that the original leader will abort in any case, so we are assisting nature: this new strong leader will carry all our blooms for the season.

Sweet peas are, as detailed above, grown on a single cordon and so are best planted one to a 7–8-foot cane, usually in rows, but they can be grown in 'wigwams' of several canes. The main task is to keep them well tied and to remove all side-shoots. With regular tying, tendrils are also best removed, thus ensuring that all the plant's energy is devoted to producing blooms.

Cultivation

Here again, an open site is by far the best. Being a legume, deep trenching is essential for the best results, incorporating lots of humus- and water-retaining material. Aim to provide a pH on the alkaline side of neutral. When applying your fertiliser, take heed of the fact that legumes possess the magical property of being able to extract nitrogen from the air and, by translocation, transfer it to the roots in the form of tiny white nodules. Therefore use a fertiliser low in nitrogen, but high in phosphates and potash.

On a personal note, I have for many years grown sweet peas on a double row approximately 24 feet long by $1\frac{1}{2}$ feet wide, using 32 plants, 16 each side, four varieties of eight. This arrangement provides me with a profusion of blooms (two cuts per week) from early June until September—a fragrant reward for my trouble.

ROSES

There have probably been more books written on roses than any other flower family, so who am I to doubt their popularity? In the late 1980s and early 1990s roses suffered a slight decline, but the new ranges of miniature, patio and ground cover roses has prompted a real upturn in their popularity. Value for money with roses is tremendous. Standard roses make an excellent focal point, giving pleasure with little pain, as they are so undemanding. Climbing roses can create a living screen of both colour and fragrance—for me half the attraction of roses is the perfume—and they make a wonderful foil for clematis. It is very rewarding to see clematis climbing through roses: two for the price of one, as no support is required for the clematis. Make sure that the varieties you choose are all of the same type as regards their pruning requirements; this will then ensure they all receive the correct treatment. Remember also that, as a bonus, the delicate seed heads of clematis are highly prized by flower arrangers and very much in demand.

Whatever the variety, roses give tremendous value for money.

The large flowers of clematis Nelly Moser give a stunning display in spring. The seed heads are attractive when the flowers have faded.

Geraniums grown in wall-pots will brighten any patio.

Alyssum will form a cushion of colour - very versatile in borders, containers and rockeries.

Impatiens, a boon for the more shady areas of the garden.

Salvia Splendens
—Blaze of Fire.‡

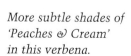

More subtle shades of
'Peaches & Cream'
in this verbena.

One of the many varieties of trailing geranium.

Trailing lobelia, a justifiably popular ingredient for hanging baskets.

SUMMER BEDDING PLANTS:
HALF-HARDY ANNUALS & HARDY ANNUALS

F1 Hybridisation

The choice of varieties of half-hardy annuals is truly enormous. The advantage of being able to plant beds of different colours, heights and shapes means that each year can offer a new vista of delight without repetition. Modern science has given us the F1 hybrids with tremendous flower power and uniformity—a far cry from my formative years. *Geraniums* that in my youth were taken as cuttings at the end of August and over-wintered in a heated greenhouse until the following May are—apart from the named varieties—a thing of the past. With the advent of F1 hybrids, seeds are now sown in February, treated with a dwarfing agent and planted out as short stocky robust plants in May, and they flower from June through to October. *Petunias* and *impatiens* ('Busy Lizzies') are perfect examples of F1 hybridisation—don't miss them.

The earliest recollections I have of 'bedders' was of *alyssum*, *lobelia*, *asters*, *snapdragons* and *salvias*. They were all good in their day and some new choice varieties are certainly still well worth growing. Plants, like fashions, have their seasons and in vogue at the moment are the wonderful F1 strains of *verbena*, *begonia multiflora*, *marigolds*, *salpiglossis*, *gazanias*, and *arctotis*. The last three are all natives of South Africa and revel in a sunny spot in a good summer. Naturally they will stand drought well, and should be more widely grown. *Zinnias* have also long been a favourite of mine, but, as a word of caution, they do not like transplanting so they are best sown singly in tiny pots or multi-cell trays to avoid root disturbance. Non-stop begonias are very popular at the moment and rightly so with their gorgeous camellia-like flowers in a great colour range. As a bonus, they make a tuber that, with care, can be dried at the end of the season and stored for next year. A case should be made for the 'new' varieties of *rudbeckia*—half hardy annual types—for they are dwarfer than the older ones and produce huge blooms late in the season to perk up the scene in late September and October.

Germinated Seedlings

The seedsmen and plant raisers are working hard for your business—and big business it most certainly is, whether you buy seed and raise your own plants or buy in the finished product for bedding out. A popular concept with all leading seedsmen is to supply, in multi-cell-trays, germinated seedlings for the buyer to grow on in a cold or frost-free greenhouse. This presents a useful cost saving, and at the same time avoids the tricky part of germination. I'm sure this will prove a winner—bedding plants without tears!

Trailing Varieties

Hanging baskets, window boxes, tubs, urns and planters, are all
designed with summer bedding in mind. These are where the trailing
or cascading varieties really come into their own. Over the last two
years I have often extolled the virtues of ***petunia surfinia***: a
revolutionary plant. Unlike the usual petunias, this is virtually
sterile and is propagated vegetatively by cuttings. Its flower power
and vigour is incredible—cascading up to four feet, covered in bloom.
Three plants will completely fill a 15-inch diameter basket. More
colour shades are being bred as I write this. The trailing varieties of
lobelia lend themselves, together with the foliage trailers of ***nepeta***,
tradescantia and ***ivy***, to being grown in baskets. Mention must also
be made of ***fuchsias*** for basket work. While these are perennial rather
than half-hardy annual or hardy annual, the colour and beauty,
together with the wide range, make them a must.

Planning

Be prepared to ring the changes on your bedding scheme, checking
the catalogues for new varieties and keeping records. Bedders are
only for one season, so you can repeat your successes and discard
your failures—I always enjoy planning my bedding plants.

A well-prepared bed—i.e. well dug and weeded with only a
minimum amount of general fertiliser at approximately two ounces
per square yard—will give a long summer display. The main
essential for a long display is regular dead-heading. This is vital, as is
an ample supply of moisture. For this I look to labour-saving
equipment such as sprinklers or the 'leaky pipe' type of flexible
porous hose that can be laid inconspicuously among the bedding
schemes. This is of course dependent on local watering restrictions.

'Dot' and 'spot' plants give flower beds both height and character
and the choice is wide. I personally use standard fuchsias as they are
so undemanding and only ask for a secure stake and a good supply of
moisture to flower profusely all summer long. These are potted,
pruned back and lifted into a greenhouse in October or November to
over-winter.

The advantages of using half-hardy annuals and hardy annuals in
the summer, followed by a spring bedding display of bulbs and
wallflowers, winter pansies, and heathers, are that you can ring the
changes in both colour, shape and form. Your displays do not become
predictable and any bare spot or failure can quickly and cheaply be
rectified. However, it must be admitted, a fair amount of work, effort
and expense is involved. With this in mind, many people
compromise by having perennials, herbaceous borders and filling in
with 'bedders' and bulbs.

Fuchsias—their colour and beauty make them a must for any garden.

Osteospermums—ideal for a sunny spot.

When choosing perennials, one should certainly do some planning as regards height, habit and colour, and any so-called permanent bed needs thorough preparation. Choice is so very wide from abutilon to zenobia, so I hesitate to make many recommendations as they are purely my own preferences. Again, modern strains of many 'golden oldies' are superb: **lupins, delphiniums, marguerites** (now re-named **argarynthemum** by the Royal Horticultural Society) can give years of pleasure. An 'oldie' back in vogue is **osteospermum** and should not be missed—my choice is **O.Whirligig**. A word of caution regarding *osteospermums*: they are not frost-hardy except in the south, so they do require cloche protection in the winter. **Fuchsias**—of which would you believe there are over 8,000 named varieties—contain many hardy varieties that make for a trouble-free display, usually still a picture well into October. A mulch of old compost, with leaf mould over the crowns in December acts as a good frost barrier, and all old stems should be left until April and then cut back to ground level.

Selecting for winter

There is no need for a garden to be dreary even in the darkest days of winter if a little careful planning and plant selection is observed. Coloured stems, bark and foliage and judicious siting can enhance a garden during the dormant winter months. Here are a few suggestions.

Winter Jasmine (Jasminum Nudiflorum). This, with its delightful sprays of yellow stars, should be in every garden. It grows to six feet high by six feet wide and can be trained up fences and walls. It can be cut in bud and will open in water.

Witch Hazel (Hamamelis Mollis). This winter beauty has convoluted flowers on bare stems (the leaves appear later). Many varieties are available, from yellow to red.

Winter Flowering Heather As distinct from the summer types of flowering heather, try the varieties *Arthur Johnson* with its pink flowers or the dark red *Myretoun Ruby*. As with all heathers, clip it over with shears after flowering.

Cornus Alba (Dogwoods). The stark-coloured crimson stems look spectacular against the snow. Try also *Cornus Alba Sibirica* with its scarlet stems, or the winter beauty *Cornus Sanguinea* with orange stems and orange autumn foliage. **NB:** prune all Cornus hard back in spring.

Bergenias. These give the most gorgeous coloured leaves, but do need a sunny site. They are a real picture when frosted. Try: *Bergenias Purpurea* with mahogany purple leaves in winter and magenta flowers on red stems in spring; *Bergenias Crassifolia* with deep red winter leaves and pink flowers in the spring; and *Bergenias Ballawley* with maroon foliage in winter and crimson flowers in the spring.

Cotoneaster Horizontalis. An evergreen, with low-growing ground cover and bright red berries.

Skimmia Japonica. Glossy foliage, white flowers and red berries.

Mahonia Japonica. The cream flowers contrast vividly with the blue foliage; it needs a sunny spot for best effect.

Helleborus Niger (Christmas Rose). I offer no apologies for including this low-growing treasure. With its showy white flowers with yellow centres, it grows to eight inches high. Cover it with a sheet of clear plastic supported on bricks (this is safer than using glass) to keep the flowers clean. It can be potted up when in bud and grown indoors. Shade will be all right, but guard against slugs.

All the above are ideal for the small or medium garden and of course a perfect complement for the next topic: bulbs.

Dogwoods, Cornus Westonbirt (red) and C. Stolonifera Flaviramea (yellow). The brightly coloured stems look spectacular in the winter.‡

Witch Hazel (Hamamelis Mollis). The convoluted flowers appear on bare stems.‡

Winter Jasmine (Jasminum Nudiflorum) provides colour in the darkest months.‡

BULBS

I always claim that bulbs are more than foolproof—virtually idiot-proof—and are a superb investment, representing excellent value if a few simple rules are followed. Always check bulbs for firmness in the base or 'plate', as it is technically called, and, irrespective of what some advertisements may say, always buy the largest size available for the best results.

Amateurs should take a leaf from the commercial bulb-grower's book when planting: namely *plant deeply*. The rule of thumb is to plant bulbs to a depth of approximately three times the diameter, so a large daffodil or tulip would need a hole of 8–9 inches. Apart from the fact that moisture is more readily available in deeper soil, there is an added bonus that the flower stems have much more rigidity and support.

Buying Bulbs

Before we consider the many types available, it should be understood that each variety has its own features of form, height and, most importantly, flowering date.

While a case can be made for buying 'mixed' daffodils or tulips as a means of economising, the resplendent colour pictures that accompany the bulbs represent a case of 'artistic licence'. Such a display cannot be achieved, simply because of the differing flowering times of the various varieties, and this is often a ploy to sell less popular or inferior bulbs. Remember the bulb-grower goes to great expense and trouble to ensure that his stock is true to his chosen variety. My firm advice is to stick to your selected variety and plant in bold clumps to achieve maximum effect.

Varieties

While the traditional yellow daffodils and red tulips are the old favourites, I do urge readers to be more adventurous and consider the vast range available today. Bulbs can, with a little planning, offer colour and beauty from January to May. With a cold frame or greenhouse, this can be extended even further, and what better to brighten the deep days of winter than a pot of vibrant colour and exotic perfume?

Prepared Bulbs

On the subject of prepared bulbs for early flowering, one immediately thinks of hyacinths, which are excellent providers of colour and perfume around Christmas time, and extremely popular. The bulbs are pre-cooled when they are bought, which ensures

Traditional favourites, daffodils and red tulips.‡

that—if planted in early September—they will be in bloom for the festive season. A golden rule with prepared bulbs is to plant only *one variety per bowl*, the reason being that, as mentioned earlier, all varieties have a different flowering date. In a container with drainage holes, use a proprietary lightweight compost, but in bowls with no holes use the so-called 'bulb fibre' to avoid the algae that form on the surface of compost when no drainage holes are present. This usually consists of peat, oyster shell and charcoal with perhaps a little base fertiliser.

The beauty of bulbs is that the flower embryo is already formed, which explains why they can flower in water jars or pebbles without any nutrients.

Hyacinths

Many colours of hyacinths are available, but for consistent results white, pink and blue varieties are by far the most reliable. (My own personal favourites are white.) For a white hyacinth, choose *L'Innocence*; for pink, *Lady Derby* (salmon pink), *Pink Pearl* (bright pink); for blue, *Delft Blue* (mid-blue), or for deep blue choose *Ostara*. Although I don't recommend reds and yellows, the best of the bunch are *Jan Bos* (red) and *City of Haarlem* (yellow).

Tulips

Certain varieties of tulip are capable of being pre-cooled to ensure early flowering. Recommended varieties include: *Marshall Joffre* (yellow); *Christmas Marvel* (rosy red); and *Brilliant Star Maximus* (dark red).

Narcissi

A few varieties of narcissi also lend themselves to the pre-cooling treatment, the pick of these being: *February Gold* (consistent yellow); *Tête-à-Tête* (delightful dwarf); *Soleil d'Or* (multi-headed, yellow and perfumed); and *Paperwhite* (white, with a fantastic perfume).

Freesias

These delightful favourites deserve a special mention. I always claim that if you are good with hyacinths you'll do well with freesias, as identical treatment is required for both plants. Freesias can be grown from seed or corm, but corm is strongly favoured. These are available in August and September and I recommend, as always, that you buy the largest size on offer. I usually pot six or seven in a five-inch pot using a peat-based compost. Plant them three inches deep and give them the 10–12-week cold treatment, as with hyacinths. Freesias

Fragrance and beauty in one from the freesia.‡

Crocus—a bulb that looks good naturalised in the lawn or in a container.‡

thrive in a cold greenhouse. Bring them in about the second week in January, if possible placing them on a high shelf, and keep them cool. A few short canes for support will be needed. The reward for your efforts is fragrance and beauty in February.

The treatment for all 'prepared' bulbs is to pot them up as early as they become available—usually in early September—and to place them in a really cool place, excluding light for 10–12 weeks. This ensures that a good strong root is formed. Bring them into the light when the top growth is approximately three inches, but *do* keep them cool, as this is the real secret of success.

Anyone with access to a reasonably dry cellar is very fortunate, as this is an ideal place to keep them for the 10–12 weeks after potting, ideally at an ambient temperature of between 5° and 7° Celsius.

A very old gardening tip that has stood the test of time is as follows. After potting, water them well and allow to drain. Scatter a few slug pellets on the surface and wrap each bowl in several thicknesses of newspaper. Dig a hole or trench a foot deep in a sheltered empty spot in the garden. Line it with bracken or straw and place the bowls in it. Cover them completely with light soil or peat, or similar, and leave them for the usual ten weeks. Then dig them up, clean the bowls, and the bulbs should be well into growth, ready for bringing into a cold greenhouse or cold-frame. Don't be alarmed by the fact that the shoots are white: they'll soon become green in the light. Only one word of caution needs to be added: do remember where you buried them!

Hanging Baskets

I have long extolled the virtues of having a winter season for your hanging basket. After all, it seems like common sense: if you already own a basket, why not have a second bite at the cherry? Clean out the old summer display in October, and top up the basket with fresh compost, then plant just one variety of dwarf tulip, or, as an alternative, one species of crocus, *iris reticulata* or *iris danfordiae*.

Tubs, urns, patio planters, and similar receptacles can all be used in the same way to make early spring a riot of colour.

BULBS FOR GARDEN USE

In order of flowering, the most popular types are as described below.

Winter Aconites

These are yellow and dwarf, and flower in January and February.

Snowdrops—the true heralders of spring.

The tiny blue flowers of Iris Reticulata 'Clairette'.‡

Snowdrops

There are many types, both double and single. Snowdrops are true heralders of spring. There is, at the time of writing, considerable controversy over snowdrops, as they are fast becoming an endangered species. They are natives of Turkey and Iran and have become a cottage industry in these countries, whereby the locals strip the hillsides and export the dried bulbs. Apart from depleting the species, the dried bulbs are often unsuccessful. The most successful way of growing snowdrops is to buy them at the end of February or early March from the specialist garden press, where they are advertised as 'in the green'. This means that the bulbs have been dug up after flowering, with all leaves and roots attached. If you plant them in a prepared site, success is virtually guaranteed. I know of many old church grounds and vicarages in Lincolnshire and Norfolk where clumps of snowdrops are sold to supplement church funds. Look out for them; they represent superb value.

Iris Reticulata and Iris Danfordiae

I am grouping these two little treasures together as they are so closely related. They both reach a height of only 3–4 inches, and flower in March if they are left outdoors, or in January and February if they are in pots and grown in a cold greenhouse or frame.

Both forms have many varieties. **_Reticulata_** is blue/mauve with contrasting coloured shoulders or 'falls'; **_Danfordiae_** is found in yellow/brown shades. All have the perfect three-petalled 'Prince of Wales' iris shape.

Puschkinia Libanotica

A small, early flower, it is silver blue and grows to three inches high. It flowers in February, and naturalises well.

Chionodoxa (Glory of the Snow)

As the name suggests, this is one of the earliest bulbs. It is lavender blue with a white eye, and spreads freely.

Crocus

Both the large-flowered and specie range are honest value-for-money bulbs that demand little effort for a super return. A hanging basket filled with a good quantity of a dark purple looks stunning on a sunny day in February.

Anemone (Wind Flower)

Here again, a wide range is available, including: **_Blanda_**, which is a very early sort and dwarf—try **_Blanda Blue_**, a bright cornflower

Snake's Head Fritillary, Fritillaria Meleagris—loves a damp shady spot.

*Another lover of moist and shade—Cyclamen Neopolitanum here
naturalised under a magnolia.‡*

colour; *St Brigid*, which is later flowering, around April, ten inches tall, and used as one of the earliest florist's cut flowers—it has a good colour range; *De Caen*, which is a single version of St Brigid; and *Fulgens*, which is scarlet red and April flowering.

NB: All anemones are dehydrated corms, so *soak them overnight* before planting them to break their dormancy. Unfortunately, most catalogues and garden centres neglect to inform buyers about this.

Allums (Ornamental Garlics)
These are members of the onion family. They can be most spectacular due to the height they attain and because of their unusual flowerheads, with the large umbels of exotic colours. The stately flowerheads of the violet-tinted variety *Giganteum* rise to four feet in height and can create a real talking point.

Fritillaria Imperialis (Crown Imperials)
This is another majestic tall plant. It easily attains three feet, with a ring of drooping bells surmounted by a pineapple foliage top. Available colours include *Rubra* (red), *Lutea* (yellow) and *Aurora* (buff). They are known to my bulb-producing friends in Spalding as 'Stinking Lilies', due to the fox-like smell of the bulbs, but don't let this put you off.

NB: The bulbs should be the size of oranges and have a large hole in one face. Plant them eight inches deep—on a handful of sand if your soil is heavy—*with the hole on the side*. It naturalises well. I cannot leave this genus of bulbs without extolling the virtues of a favourite of mine. In the same family as the 'Crown Imperials', *Fritillaria Meleagris* is commonly known as 'The Snake's Head Fritillary'. It only grows eight inches tall, and the nodding heads, from which it derives its name, are veined purple and white. It loves a shady damp spot.

Daffodils and Narcissi
These are all, botanically speaking, belonging to the genus *narcissi*. They are grouped by the National Daffodil Society into different sections or, as they prefer, 'divisions', ranging from Division 1 to Division 10. I strongly urge anyone with a real interest to join the National Daffodil Society—but then, all specialist societies have so much to offer, with local branches and meetings where people with a common interest meet both socially and to improve their knowledge.

Specialist growers issue comprehensive catalogues well worth studying, but beware as some of the rarer varieties can cost several pounds per bulb. It is very easy to fall prey to what the enthusiasts call 'yellow fever' and run riot in your purchasing.

The range of colours of daffodils becomes wider and more exotic every year. Whilst yellow is the traditional colour, you might like to consider the pinks, reds and orange cups that are now widely grown, or the delicate rimmed varieties. Double forms are really flamboyant, but have one inherent problem: in a wet season the heads can become top-heavy. Many of the multi-headed species provide a bonus with their splendid perfume, and are usually late-flowering, thus extending the season into May.

Tulips

It is 400 years since the first tulips arrived in this country from Holland, and they're still going strong. As with daffodils, a vast range of colour, types and flowering dates is available. The dwarf species and rockery types give a warm glow to late winter, and among my personal favourites I urge you to try *Tarda*, which is only 2–3 inches high, multi-headed, yellow with white tips and naturalises well. *Praestan's Fusilier* is another safe bet—again it is multi-headed, five inches tall and a glowing vermilion red. These can be followed by all the various colours of the taller *Darwin* and *Triumph* tulips. When they are mass-planted with wall flowers, they create a spectacular show.

GARDEN PLANTING & CULTIVATION OF BULBS

While stable manure is usually the gardener's favourite source of humus, care must be taken of its use in bulb cultivation. Bulbs are easily 'burnt' by manure unless it's at least two years old; a safer alternative is well-rotted garden compost. The main criterion is to plant to the correct depth: eight inches is a good general guide for larger bulbs such as daffodils and tulips. Fertiliser is required both for improving the quality of the bloom, and, more importantly, building up the following year's flowers. Nitrogenous fertilisers should be used with great caution, the main requirement being phosphates and potash, the root and flower builders. Too much nitrogen can induce soft bulbs and the dreaded 'base rot'.

Dead-heading is a must, but allow the foliage to die down for at least 6–8 weeks after flowering. A couple of liquid feeds, using a high-potash ratio, while the leaves are still green and turgid after dead-heading, does wonders for next season's crop. Both daffodils and tulips can be left *in situ* unless the area is required for summer bedding: you only need to lift and divide them when the clump becomes crowded or ceases to perform satisfactorily. Lifting and dividing is best carried out in June during the dormant season. Should you need to lift bulbs to make way for summer bedding, just try to lift them with all the foliage and root attached, plant them in an odd corner to the same depth, water well and give them a liquid feed or two. After the foliage dies down, lift them and store in a cool and dry place ready for replanting in autumn. It sounds a lot of trouble, but it's well worth the effort.

Diseases

Base rot is the most common problem with bulbs, but good garden hygiene, coupled with rigorous selection of stock, is more than half the battle. When planting, a pre-dipping in a good fungicide, coupled with a dusting of BHC dust in the planting hole, gets them off to a flying start.

Pests

The **narcissi fly**—or rather its progeny the *grub*—can do untold damage and is often blamed for bulbs going blind, in other words not producing any flowers. Any infected bulbs should be removed and burnt, but the use of a good garden pesticide at planting time should act as a deterrent, along with an annual dusting of pesticide at shoot emergence time.

    Regarding so-called 'blind' bulbs, I am often asked why it occurs. Apart from the obvious narcissi fly grub, the answer is usually concerned with feeding bulbs after flowering, or, more precisely, neglecting to do so. It is a simple rule, but one that must be followed: *feed after flowering for the next season's flowers.*

SUMMER BULBS

Strictly speaking, not all the subjects covered in this section are actually bulbs by a botanical definition, but they deserve mention nonetheless.

Agapanthus

In the cold northern climate, the umbels of the most bewitching cornflower blue need a little nursemaiding to become established, but when this is achieved, they are best left undisturbed. They make a splendid foil in any border. They like a moist humus-rich site, and, for the first year or so, a cloche in winter is well advised.

Cannas

This is a native of South Africa, providing exotic warm colours and interesting shapes in August. They need lifting for the winter.

Chincherinchees

This is another native of South Africa. The sap from the bulb is used

An impressive display of gladioli.‡

in the medical profession as a treatment for certain types of heart diseases, and for this reason it was taken off the market for some years so stocks could be built up. With a delicate column of white stars tapering to a point, its main claim to fame is that it lasts an astonishing six weeks as a cut flower.

Ranunculus
The newer strains have an exciting colour range and are ideal for borders or tubs. They have strange-looking claw-like tubers: these claws should be planted downwards in April.

Cyclamen Neapolitanum
A fully hardy outdoor subject, it loves semi-shade and being kept moist. Once established, it will flourish for years.

Begonias
The tuberous types of begonia are highly recommended, as they are so accommodating. The pendula types look stunning cascading from hanging baskets or urns, while the upright types make ideal central focal points for tubs and window boxes. They also look excellent bedded out, which is my preferred location for them. Small hardwood stakes are needed to support the taller varieties, as both the stems and blooms are quite heavy. Store the tubers dry in a frost-free shed or greenhouse over winter, after dusting with sulphur powder.

Gladioli
This family of flowers has won some very ardent enthusiasts. The keen grower plants them in straight rows for ease of cultivation and religiously stakes out each spike: this is the correct method for exhibiting or simply to get the best results for use as cut flowers. However, they can also be grown and shown to great effect when planted in clumps of somewhere between five and nine corms at the rear of beds, borders or dwarf shrubs. A little judicious staking will help, but the natural curve of wind-blown flower spikes adds to their charm.

Gladioli can be classified into three main types: large-flowered; 'primulinus' or 'butterfly'; and small-flowered—each with its own particular appeal. Again, specialist suppliers exist, and are recommended for the serious gardener who is looking for that little extra. Cultivars are bred in such diverse locations as Australia, North America, the UK, Czechoslovakia and, of course, Holland. There are literally hundreds of named varieties and a visit to a national show when a sea of blooms are displayed is an awesome sight. If you visit one, take along a notebook and camera.

Cultivation

Deeply-dug land with good drainage is the main criterion, and once they begin growing, constant watering is essential. On heavy land, settling the corms on a handful of sand is advisable to prevent corm rot before new roots are formed. A sunny site is also of the essence. During a growing season—usually from April to October—the gladiolus corm is a real powerhouse of energy, fulfiling three functions: supplying a glorious flower spike; producing a new corm for the following season; and producing a quantity of cormlets or 'fry', which, if grown on for three seasons, will also produce full-size flowering corms.

After flowering, the foliage should be left and the corm fed with a high-potash liquid feed to plump up the new corms. Dig them up towards the end of October as the foliage dies down; dry them fairly quickly and remove the newly-formed corm for next year. Remove the cormlets as well if you wish to grow these on. Store the corms in dry conditions at around 7° Celsius. Dust them with flowers of sulphur to prevent base rot.

Fertiliser

A good general fertiliser of blood fish and bone, or Growmore, at two ounces per square yard is fine, and remember that gladioli respond well to liquid feeding.

Pests and Diseases

The main enemy of the gladiolus family is **thrip**, which is easily recognisable by the white zig-zag pattern made in the leaf blades. Again, prevention is better than cure: a suitable routine spray with a systemic insecticide every fourteen days should keep these enemies at bay. A dusting with a soil insecticide on planting should deter wireworm and keep your crop clean.

Varieties

There are too many varieties to mention, but below is my own selection for anyone fairly new to gladiolus growing and looking for something interesting, but readily available and not extortionately priced.

Large-flowering types

Drama. Watermelon pink with a yellow throat.
Esta Bonita. Apricot-coloured and huge, sometimes reaching six feet;
Lowland Queen. Yellow with cerise blotches.
Royal Dutch. Which is self lavender.

Primulinus and small-flowered types
Columbine. Which is pink and white—an old favourite, but still
    great.
Red Jewel. Which is scarlet with a white line, and very eye-catching.
Georgette. Which is orange/yellow.
Spring Green. Which is a little green gem—floral art students go
    wild over this one!

Columbine looking pretty in the border.

A friable light soil is the ideal for producing carrots.‡

Vegetables

All sorts of roots and herbs in gardens grow,
Parsnips, carrots, turnips or what you'll sow.
Onions, melons, cucumbers, radishes,
Skirrets, beets, coleworts and fair cabbages.

W. Bradford

THERE IS NO EXCUSE for not growing at least some edible crop, irrespective of how small your plot is. As I've already mentioned, with nothing more than growbags, tubs, urns, or even hanging baskets, vegetables can be produced. The main three reasons for growing vegetables, apart from the creative satisfaction, are, I believe, as follows:

1. Nothing can beat home-grown produce for freshness.
2. We pick them young, so the flavour is unbeatable.
3. The amateur grows varieties for taste, not necessarily for the highest yield as the professional farmer or grower does.

FLOWER BEDS AND BORDERS

While there are many practical advantages in devoting at least a part of the garden to vegetables, they can also be quite at home, with careful selection, in the flower beds and borders. Taking a closer look at this proposal, consider the following points in its favour:

Carrots
The fern-like foliage looks very attractive when small clumps appear among our flower borders, and they will certainly hold their own as items of interest.

Beetroot
Again, the strikingly-marked red and green broad leaves, often with heavy ribbing, contrast well with coltness bedding dahlias in particular. If you try it, I'm sure you'll be delighted with the result.

The author in his greenhouse with a good crop of tomatoes.

Runner Beans

A wigwam of 6–8 canes placed at the rear of borders provides both height, colour and an edible bonus. The leaf is quite attractive, and when in flower both the red- and white-seeded varieties look appealing.

TUBS, URNS AND WINDOW BOXES

These can all look attractive and provide fresh produce at the same time. Short-rooted subjects with the emphasis on fairly quick-maturing varieties should be the ones to choose.

Herbs

Herbs lend themselves to container work and to hanging baskets. A basket or tub containing several varieties of mint gives the cook both choice and a fresh supply. Place the tub near the kitchen door for added convenience.

Tomatoes

I must mention a fairly new variety that has earned its spurs in hanging baskets, and that is F1 hybrid *Tumbler*. It is a short-jointed cascading plant that is a joy both to grow and admire. The foliage is emerald green, and the yellow, star-like flowers are followed by fruit that changes from dark green to nearly white, orange and finally to bright red. And there is a taste to match the visual appeal of the bite-size fruit.

An added bonus of using hanging baskets is the absence of slugs and soil-borne pests. Watering very frequently is the main task, but if you use water-retaining granules in the compost, this will really lighten the load.

GROWBAGS

At the last count, the number of growbags produced in 1994 was estimated at over seven million, with prices ranging from 64p to over £2. The first growbags became popular for producing tomato crops in the amateur greenhouse: because of a gradual build-up of diseases and, in border growing, soluble salts, tomato-growing had become impracticable. By using growbags the crop is isolated from the disease present in the greenhouses and borders.

Growbags do offer quite reasonable results, but watering can become a problem. They can be used successfully for melons, courgettes, cucumbers, peppers and so on, and as an added bonus the spent contents makes a good mulch at the end of the season around shrubs and bushes. It is *not* recommended to attempt a second main crop in a used growbag, although winter lettuce and radish are possibilities after a little general fertiliser is added to replenish the exhausted original feed.

THE OUTDOOR VEGETABLE GARDEN

While all aspects of gardening can and should be a pleasure, it is worthwhile remembering the practical considerations of cost, effort, land occupied and yield. One should always consider whether the end result is worth the work and the expense.

As a very young naïve gardener, I remember the advice given by the so called 'senior' pundits when I took over a new virgin site. I was advised to 'plant spuds—nothing will break the land up better'. Actually, nothing could be further from the truth. Cultivating potatoes involves: (i) digging and trenching the land to plant; (ii) earthing up the growing crop (a further digging operation); and (iii) digging again to harvest the crop. In a four-month period, therefore, the plot has been worked three times. Apart from the low value of potatoes, they are voracious feeders and denude the land of most nutrients.

Having said that, I would never stop growing them entirely, but I restrict myself to 'first earlies' grown under a floating cloche of horticultural fleece. This gives me really early new potatoes in May from a March planting.

LEGUMES

The legume family (peas and beans) possesses a most unusual inherent characteristic, namely that they can extract nitrogen from the air and, by the process of translocation, transfer it to the roots where it is stored as tiny white nodules. This amazing ability means that the plants are generating their own supply of nitrogen, so when choosing a fertiliser one should aim for a blend that is high in phosphates and potash but low in nitrogen. A pH on the alkaline side of neutral, around 7.5, is perfect.

> *I always eat peas with honey,*
> *I've done it all my life,*
> *They do taste kind of funny,*
> *But it keeps them on my knife.*
>
> Anon

Runner Beans

I always maintain that for value for money and for economy of
space, runner beans easily come out on top. The most usual method
of growing them is either in wigwams made of 6–8-foot canes tied
together at the top, or in straight double rows—again with eight-foot
canes—and braced at each end with poles and plastic wire.
Whichever way you choose, plant your beans on the *inside* of your
canes. I suggest we assist nature by sowing seeds individually in
either small pots or multi-cell trays. They transplant well, but
remember that runner beans are *frost-sensitive*, and thus cannot be
planted out until early June, hence the reason for pot-sowing. A cold
greenhouse or cold-frame is ideal, but if neither is available, a
temporary structure can easily be concocted with bricks and a glass,
or clear plastic, cover. Position it in a sheltered semi-shaded spot
outside. Sow your seeds in early May and by early June young sturdy
plants will be ready for planting out. Rich, moisture-retaining land is
needed and should be kept well watered.

Setting of the flowers can sometimes be a problem should a cold
windy period arise: this usually happens in early August. Many tips
have been proffered on this subject, and one of the most common
ones—which I hesitate to recommend—is to spray the open flowers
with cold water. Now this may work if you use tepid water with a
very fine mist in early evening, but I remember seeing one old
allotment gardener blasting the flowers with a fierce spray from an
old stirrup pump: the ground was littered with shattered flowers. A
far better suggestion, and one much more in harmony with the
course of nature, is to pour a strong sugar solution into two or three
old jam jars and place them along your bean rows. They will attract
the bees who will carry out the pollination for you.

Varieties

Runner beans are generally grown with two ends in mind: for the
pot; and for showing. My preferred varieties are **As Long as Your
Arm** and **Yardstick**, both of good taste and vigour. However, a new
variety that I have trialled with success is **Lady Di**, which produces
broad flat beans with an excellent flavour that does not go 'beany',
and they can achieve show length.

Dwarf Beans

Commonly referred to as 'French Beans', dwarf beans take up more
space, only growing 8–9 inches high, but producing the most
succulent-tasting beans. They need to be grown fast, without any
check, and picked frequently. They make a great crop in a growbag
either in a greenhouse or standing on a warm sheltered paved area. It

Runner beans—a crop giving great value for money and economy of space.‡

is a real connoisseur's vegetable, but *frost-tender*. My suggested variety is the old but well-proven **The Prince**.

Broad Beans

Unlike the other more delicate beans, broad beans are as tough as old boots, but are really tender and tasty and a joy to eat. Like all vegetables, pick them young and enjoy a taste *par excellence*.

After my 'first early' spuds in May, broad beans are the next earliest main vegetable crop to be harvested—usually in mid-June. This is achieved by always sowing the beans in individual pots in a frost-free greenhouse in early January. (This is another opportunity for me to remind you about the importance of keeping a gardening diary, so that you don't miss the planting dates.) The pots produce sturdy plants for planting out in mid to late March, subject to conditions being favourable. Cloches can be used to advantage on really exposed snowy sites, but don't forget that these beans are tough. However, I suggest you stake them with a 2–3-foot cane against wind rock.

Catalogues often suggest that certain varieties can be sown outdoors in October or November and over-wintered, but I've always found my January greenhouse sowing gives perfect results. For outdoor autumn sowing, set a few extra seeds at the end of each row to fill in any gaps—this ensures full, neat rows!

Pests and Diseases

Chocolate Spot is easily recognised as its name aptly describes the symptom. It is a fungal airborne disease that looks unsightly and has a debilitating effect on the yield—but not drastically. Use a good systemic fungicide and change your site annually.

Slugs can be a problem when tender young beans are planted in situ in March, so take the usual precautions.

Black Fly is the most well-known and most feared broad bean pest, however, these do not have to be the scourge that so many gardeners believe them to be. The deterrent is simple. The 'protected' sowing method in January, followed by the planting-out of sturdy plants in March, produces a good flush of flowers in May. Once a good number of flowers are on each stem, *pinch out the top*. This has two effects: (i) the flowers that the plant produces set early beans, as all the plant's energy is diverted to the flowers once the growing point has been removed; and (ii) black fly do not usually appear till late May and always congregate on the succulent top, which is no longer there, so they fly elsewhere.

Varieties

Both white- and green-seeded varieties are available. ***Imperial Green Longpod*** has an excellent flavour, but is rather tall; ***Jubilee Hysor*** is white-seeded, and also tall, but superb both for table and exhibition, carrying up to nine beans per pod. ***The Sutton*** is bred for the small plot or can even be grown in a container or growbag. It grows to only $1\frac{1}{2}$ feet with six-inch mini-pods.

Peas

The Rolls Royce of garden vegetables, a serving of fresh garden peas is a true delight. With all due respect to our commercial veg grower, the 'field' type of pea bears no resemblance to the varieties and taste produced by the amateur gardener. The reason is obvious: we pick them while they are young, and if they are gathered and cooked within one hour, their exquisite sweetness is retained.

Peas are better grown in rows, in a slightly alkaline soil, with lots of moisture-retaining material in the bottom of the trenches. Being a legume, little nitrogen is required, but phosphates and potash should be the order of the day. The finest row of peas I ever grew was in a deeply-trenched row into which I incorporated a large quantity of rotted leaves in the bottom. This acted as a moisture reservoir and the results were amazing. This experience taught me that peas need a copious supply of water and it is a lesson I have always tried to follow.

Peas are available in three main types: earlies, mid-season and late varieties, and a very good suggestion is to start with an early variety, obviously, but also to finish your season with an early variety. 'Earlies' mature approximately twelve weeks from sowing, so a late sowing—around the end of July—can give a final crop of peas in mid-October. By sowing in succession from March, they can be harvested from June to October. Heights vary, but I always support the plants with either pea sticks or nets.

Pests and Diseases

Spray against the ***pea maggot*** and also against the ***pea aphid***. Do this after the flowers have set, but before the pods fill. Late-sown peas are, unfortunately, susceptible to ***mildew***, particularly in cold damp autumns; this is why the last crop, to be really successful, should be harvested by the end of October. A systemic fungicide helps to ward off mildew.

Varieties

Earlies take twelve weeks to mature. The ***Early Onward*** is $2\frac{1}{2}$ feet tall and very sweet. The tried and tested ***Kelvedon Wonder*** is dwarf. at $1\frac{1}{2}$ feet high. Of mid-season varieties, ***Onward*** matures two weeks after Early Onward, and ***Hurst Greenshaft*** is two feet tall with large pods.

Maincrop varieties include: ***Alderman***, a tall variety at five feet, but prolific and good. ***Show Perfection*** is my personal favourite, with thin-shelled pods containing up to twelve peas each. It is a top show-winner with a taste to match, and tall, achieving 5–6 feet.

Snap Peas or Mange Tout are becoming even more popular. Among the wide range available, try: ***Dwarf Sweet Green***, which is quite dwarf at approximately two feet and has a high sugar content; or ***Orgegon Sugar Pod***, the RHS-selected variety, which is recommendation enough.

BRASSICAS

> *A cauliflower is a cabbage with a college education.*
>
> Mark Twain

The brassica family includes a large proportion of our staple diet of greens, and is grown in profusion. The British climate suits most members of this family extremely well, from spring greens to winter sprouts. Before we explore the various types, a few general observations are in order. One tried and tested maxim from my youth was: to test the quality of a new garden, plant cauliflowers. Nothing else proves the quality of your plot more accurately than caulies. I've given and used this advice for years and it's never let me down. I have seen cabbage flourish and cauli do poorly, which bears the old maxim out.

All brassicas enjoy a fairly high pH, so use lime if your reading is below 7.0. Also, and this cannot be overemphasised, *plant firmly*. I personally stake my sprouts to obviate wind rock. Loose planting, and hence loose plants, is the prime reason for sprouts 'blowing' or not making buttons.

Below is some of the most important information regarding the health and well-being of your brassicas.

Disease

Club-root, also referred to as 'Finger and Thumb Disease' in parts of East Anglia is the main disease to affect Brassicas. Its symptoms are roots which become twisted and arthritic and a plant that is stunted and deformed. It is often said that once club-root is in a plot it takes at least ten years to eradicate it. This sounds very pessimistic, but don't despair, we can succeed.

Crop rotation is vital, even if you only move your site a few feet every year.

Raise Your Own Plants. My apologies to the nurserymen for depriving them of business, but I strongly recommend raising your own plants. The reason for this is to produce 'clean' plants in splendid isolation in pots and cell-trays with sterile, fresh, growing compost. On infected land I've seen quite good results obtained by raising plants in this way, then potting into five-inch pots and planting out with an obvious large root mass and compost. This means that the crop is virtually contained within its own specially-prepared, sterile environment.

Liming deters club-root, and brassicas thrive in a high-pH environment.

Armillatox is a gardener's multi-purpose friend. Of its many uses, not least is as a good deterrent, rather than a cure, for club-root. It is widely used by brassica growers and exhibitors.

By following the above suggestions I'm convinced club-root can be kept to a minimum. I personally never plant any brassica plant that I have not raised, to avoid the risk of importing the dreaded disease.

Pests

The main threats to brassicas are ***cabbage root fly caterpillar*** and ***aphids***. The cabbage white butterfly, although it looks attractive, is the precursor of the grub and caterpillar that can wreak havoc. Good systemic insecticides are available, and I advise doubling up on these, in other words using two products in rotation, as pests can build up an immunity. I must reiterate that prevention is better than cure, so early preventative spraying is advisable. A very old remedy that holds true is to spray brassicas with a very weak solution of Jeyes Fluid, at one teaspoonful per gallon. The theory is that the smell is offensive to the cabbage white butterfly, so they will not settle and lay their eggs. Netting of course has much to commend it, but don't shut the stable door when the horse has bolted—net before the first butterfly is seen.

Cabbage

A staple English traditional vegetable, the cabbage is worthy of more recognition. With careful planning, the home gardener can achieve a supply of cabbage virtually all the year round. Be aware that the F1 hybrid types are available for all seasons and give consistently good

Not an easy crop to grow, the cauliflower tests a gardener's skills.‡

A traditional vegetable, with careful planning cabbage can be enjoyed all year round.‡

results. Choosing your variety is very much a question of taste, but certain ones stand out.

F1 hybrid *Hispi* is a true summer cabbage from a spring sowing. Its conical shape is small and therefore ideal for the small family, and it can be grown closely spaced. It has a delicious flavour and is non-bolting. F1 hybrid *Minicole* is a round variety that stands well. It is also small in size but big in quality. F1 hybrid *Tundra* is sown in summer and harvested in winter. It has an excellent texture and stands the winter well.

For the earliest spring cabbage try *Pixie*, which is not an F1 hybrid but one of the earliest and most reliable of spring greens. Sow it in August or September and it will be ready in March.

Cauliflower

The cauliflower is the test of the gardener's skill and quality of his soil. They like plenty of water and *firm* planting. Give them plenty of space to mature—approximately $2\frac{1}{2}$ feet all round, for the main types. Like cabbages, F1 Hybrids have really taken over and currently hold sway. Many varieties originate from Australia, where extensive cauliflower breeding and development has been carried out.

Suggested varieties are: the tried and tested *Dok Elgon*, which is an early variety that matures thirteen weeks from planting; the F1 hybrid *Elby*, which is large, succulent and very vigorous, maturing in early autumn from a spring sowing; *Barrier Reef*, which as you might imagine originates from 'down under', and is well proven as a late-October/early-November variety.

With all cauliflowers, rich fertile land is needed and no checks during the growing period. As the curds develop it is a good idea to crack two or three of the outer leaves and bend them over to ensure a clean white cauliflower.

Sprouts

No Christmas feast would be complete without a dish of steaming sprouts as a staple vegetable to accompany the turkey and all its trimmings. As with cauliflower, F1 hybrids are virtually essential; in fact the commercial brassica growers have used F1 hybrid varieties exclusively for more than a decade. There is a wide choice of varieties, but by far the number one for home gardeners must be the F1 hybrid *Peer Gynt*. It matures from September onwards, and is dwarf in height, thus avoiding wind rock, a problem with tall varieties. It excels in both taste and yield. F1 hybrid *Fortress* is ideal to follow on from *Peer Gynt*. It is winter-hardy and lasts until March. With a few plants of the above two varieties, a small family can enjoy sprouts from early September until late March.

When gathering, crop a few buttons off each plant, always from the bottom upwards, and consider staking each plant. While sprouts are free-standing, two of the main reasons for 'blown' sprouts or loose buttons are loose planting and wind rock. Staking goes a very long way to ensuring firm sprouts.

Chinese Cabbage

While discussing brassicas, consideration should be given to the ever-increasing demand and popularity of Chinese Cabbage. Most are ideal for close planting, and lend variety to your meals, either as salad ingredients, as a boiled vegetable, or, as many prefer, as a stir-fry. Varieties are appearing in an incessant stream from the plant breeders: it remains to be seen which prove the most popular. The growbag or patio container can be used to good effect here.

MINI-VEG

Another type of vegetable that is currently in vogue is the fast-growing range of mini-veg. Obviously aimed at the smaller family, they again recommend themselves to the gardener without a garden! Tubs, planters and even window-boxes can be successfully pressed into service. Close spacing is the order of the day and, being small, waste is cut to a minimum. Most seedsmen now list a complete family of mini-veg, and I'm convinced we will hear much more of these over the next few years as their popularity increases. From my own experience, below are some mini-veg that I think are here to stay and will stand the test of time.

Suggested Varieties

Beetroot. I suggest two new varieties, both producing ping-pong-ball-size baby beet: Detroit 2—*Nero* or *Monaco*.

Cauliflower. Two that will do you proud are *Lateman* and *Idol*. They serve one or two people.

Cabbage. Try F1 hybrid *Castello* as a ball-shaped cabbage, or F1 hybrid *Protovy*, which is a Savoy type, and much later in the season.

Carrot. Baby carrots are always a delight, either cooked or in salads. Try *Amini* or *Minicor*.

Onion. For your summer salads try a special new colour: a spring onion that is mild but an intense deep red shade, called *Redmate*.

Leek. A new extra-mild variety called *King Richard* is grown as a spring bunching onion. Pull when young, at pencil thickness.

Turnip. F1 hybrid *Tokyo Cross* has a white tiny globular shape. Cook it or use in salads.

Onions—a vital ingredient in almost any recipe.‡

Courgette. I reckon the pick of the 'minis' are F1 hybrid ***Supremo*** or ***Ambassador***. In both cases harvest when 3–4 inches long.

Kohl Rabi. This makes another addition to your summer salad. ***Logo*** and ***Roland*** are two new varieties that both mature in 8–9 weeks under reasonable conditions.

Tomatoes. The premier variety for ease of cultivation and for use in hanging baskets must be F1 hybrid ***Tumbler***. It really excels in both habit and yield. However, a new variety that performs well in containers is ***Brasero***, which has small sweet fruit. It has a self-branching habit and a good reputation and background.

ONIONS

> *This is every cooks opinion,*
> *No savoury dish without an onion,*
> *But lest your kissing should be spoiled,*
> *Your onions must be thoroughly boiled.*
>
> Swift

Onions are the delight of both our finest chefs and the keen exhibition vegetable grower. Visit any show from the tiniest hamlet to the national exhibitions and the crowds flock around the onion exhibits. The onion family, or *allium*, to give it its botanical name, comes in many guises, but basically the bulb onion is by far the widest-used vegetable. Open any recipe book to confirm this.

Whole volumes have been written on the cultivation of onions, but for the average gardener looking for a good crop, growing can be quite simple. They like an open situation, a reasonable depth of soil free of stones, and they should be fed with a fairly high phosphate and potash fertiliser. Onions can be grown in two different formats, as explained below.

Onion Sets

These are in fact mini-onion plants which, by the wonders of modern science, are virtually held in a state of suspended animation ready to burst into growth when planted. Produced by specialists, they are grown from seed then very carefully dried and stored at an exact temperature. I always refer to onion sets as being 'idiot-proof', as all they ask is to be planted in March or April and off they go. What could be simpler?

One of the main advantages of sets becomes apparent after harvesting, as it is an accepted fact that onions grown this way keep better than their illustrious big brothers grown from seed. One of the few problems associated with onion sets is that, after planting, they are often found uprooted and scattered around for no apparent reason. The culprits are birds collecting material to build their nests. The dry chaff-like neck of an onion set looks ideal, but when they tug at it they find a small onion at the end and thus discard it in favour of more suitable items. The simple way to prevent this, and to produce full uniform rows, is to plant onion sets in trays or boxes of lightweight compost under glass—either a greenhouse or cold-frame. Plant them in February, and by the end of March they are growing nicely with green tops and a good root system ready for planting out. Plant them out in rows six inches apart with six inches between bulbs.

As far as varieties are concerned, for years **Stuttgarten** was the mainstay of sets, but recently bigger and better strains have become available, notably **Ailsa Craig**. Yes, the seed show onion of yesteryear is now available as a set. **Sturon** is very reliable and a good cropper with a mild flavour. **Turbo** is better-shaped, and has show potential in the eight-ounce class.

Onions from Seed

These have been grown to over fourteen pounds, with 'tops and tails'—a far cry from only 1987 when the world record stood at a little over seven pounds.

There is no real mystique in growing large onions—the skill is in the giant ones. To grow sound large onions to about 4–5 pounds, a good technique, a long season of growth, and the right varieties will put you well along the path to success.

Ideally they should be sown in gentle heat very early in the season. January is ideal if you can provide a mini-warm environment of 65–70° Fahrenheit to aid germination. A small electrical propagator or a soil warming cable will be very helpful here. Once germinated and pricked off into cell trays or small pots, the temperature can be dropped to approximately 50° Fahrenheit. Allow maximum exposure to light and air on all possible occasions. Do not be in too great a hurry to plant them out: after all, while they are happily growing in the greenhouse you can carry on preparing the beds for when the weather becomes suitable.

Basically, onions love a deep humus-rich soil with plenty of old well-rotted stable manure mixed in. Plant them out in late April when the seedlings should be growing strongly. Ensure that they are well hardened off before planting, and don't worry if this is delayed due to uncertainties in the weather.

Pests and Diseases

Onions remain surprisingly free of pest damage, but their main problem is fungal diseases, particularly **base rot** and **neck rot**. The method of combating these is to practise soil sterilisation of your beds. Armillatox and Jeyes Fluid are the obvious choices here, and a good systemic fungicide should be used from the seed-sowing stage.

Harvesting

When harvesting, it is very good practice to bend the tops over when it is apparent that growth has virtually stopped. Carefully insert a fork near each onion, and gently lever upwards until the tap root is broken, after which the onion will begin to ripen.

There are many ways of drying the onions. The main criterion is that it must be done thoroughly to ensure good storage. An old but successful method is to pile the onions in a small heap in the sunniest spot of your garden and place a cloche over them. Turn them regularly and don't store them until they are completely dry. Alternatively, if a greenhouse is available, place the onions on a staging, again turning frequently.

Varieties

For the home gardener the choice is vast. The following will all produce large bulbs—up to exhibition size with a little extra attention to detail. **Ailsa Craig** is an oldie, and the yardstick by which all onions are judged. It has been used in the breeding of many new show-winning strains. **Lancastrian** is another oldie that is now back in vogue. It can produce five-pound bulbs quite easily and has a very mild flavour. **Bedfordshire Champion** keeps well and has a solid texture.

Spring and Salad Onions

These are usually grown as a 'catch crop' in any good corner, but are invaluable in salads. Sow a pinch regularly for succession. Among the better varieties are: **White Lisbon**, which has been the standard variety since time immemorial, but to lend added colour and variety to your salad bowl grow the new dark red variety **Redmate**, which I mentioned earlier.

LEEKS

Leeks are the obvious vegetable to discuss after onions, as they are closely related. Their main claim to fame—apart from their exalted place on the show bench—is that, unlike onions, they do not need lifting, drying and storing, but can be used directly from the ground.

Beetroot a fairly easy crop to grow.‡

There are two basic types of leek: the 'blanch leek' with its long straight shaft; and the 'pot leek', which is short—a blanched portion is usually no longer than six inches—and is very fat and stocky. Both types have a mild flavour and can be used in a variety of ways. The long blanch type will give a much longer blanched edible portion if it is covered with plastic or clay pipes of a suitable diameter and length as they grow. Soil and cultivation for all types of leeks is the same as it is for onions: a rich friable soil with as much depth as possible. A raised bed gives superb results if you have the time and inclination.

Pests and Diseases

As with onions, pests are not a problem, but leeks can suffer from a virus disease commonly referred to as *rust*. Its symptom is a brown, rusty discoloration on the blanched portion. Strict hygiene is the order here: change your beds and use systemic fungicides to keep it in check.

Varieties

Musselburgh is an old variety, but reliable; *Lyon Prizetaker* is long, tender and very mild; *King Richard* is a newer variety, which is late maturing.

BEETROOT

Beetroot is one of the garden's standby vegetables, and not too demanding in its requirements. Avoid using fresh manure as this causes 'fanging' or 'forking' of the roots. It does not take kindly to transplanting, except when using module trays and sowing and transplanting with great care. When planting outdoors, sow them in rows as thinly as possible and remove weaker seedlings. During the growing season a light dusting of kitchen or table salt improves the flavour dramatically. When harvesting, a good tip is to twist off the tops rather than using a knife as this reduces bleeding.

Beetroots are available as either globe-shaped or tapering, and many new varieties are becoming available that are well worth investigating. Tried and tested varieties include: *Boltardy*, the standard by which all beetroot are judged; *Detroit*, an early type; and F1 hybrid *Red Ace*, a new hybrid that is proving very reliable.

CARROTS

Carrots are another root crop that give a good account of themselves in most situations. A sandy, friable bed is ideal, with very few stones or rubble; otherwise roots may become distorted.

Basically, there are two main types of carrot: the stump-rooted and the long. Stump-rooted are by far the best for shallow land and are essential for growbag cultivation. Sow them thinly and remember, as mentioned earlier, small clumps can look both attractive and be productive in your flower borders.

The main enemy of this vegetable is the dreaded carrot root fly. The best defence is to cover your rows with 'floating' fleece for the first three weeks in May when this menace is on the wing and looking for a home. Also, when thinning the seedlings, make sure you disturb the soil as little as possible and remove all the discarded seedlings.

Several new strains of carrot have recently become available, including F1 hybrid *Fly Away* and F1 hybrid *Vigor*. Bred specifically to be immune from the ravages of carrot fly, and they have a good flavour. *Early Nantes* is a long, tapering reliable variety; and *Autumn King* is a stump-rooted late variety with a heavy yield.

PARSNIPS

One always associates parsnips with roast beef, as they complement each other so well. As with all root vegetables, deep beds give the best results and similar conditions to carrots are ideal. Many gardeners claim that the flavour is improved after they have been frosted, so parsnips make a very valuable late root vegetable. Canker is its only main problem, but many varieties are resistant to it, such as *Avon Resister*. The premier variety is, however, *Tender and True*, with many show awards to its name. A first F1 hybrid has received glowing reports; it is called *Gladiator* and is well worth seeking out.

CELERY

Giant strides have been made with celery, again thanks to the plant breeders, in producing new self-blanching strains. The original types are all grown in very rich trenches, then earthed up as growth becomes rapid. Success in the shape of crisp succulent sticks of celery is achieved by plenty of water, and, when the celery is growing strongly, use a high-nitrogen liquid feed, ideally with a ratio of 3–0–1 or 4–1–2.

Slugs are celery's worst enemy, so take steps to eradicate them. I personally find a liquid slug bait very effective.

Trench varieties—which require blanching with brown paper or corrugated paper—include: *Ideal*, which is old, reliable, and a top show-winner; and *Giant Pink*, a tall variety that is pale pink in colour. Of the self-blanching types, choose F1 hybrid *Victoria*, an early type that is green and quick-growing, and, I predict, is set to become better known and more popular; and *Celebrity*, which crops in autumn outdoors, but is very useful in a cold greenhouse for summer use.

CUCUMBERS

In my formative years in gardening, the only cucumbers one ever grew were either 'Telegraph' or 'Butcher's Disease Resistant'. Alas, they are nearly things of the past. In the early days of F1 hybridisation, cucumber growing really took off with the advent of the F1 all-female types. I always describe these by saying 'there's a chicken in every egg', because they only produce female flowers—with the tiny embryo fruit behind—and no males. This ensures that fertilisation cannot take place, so the days of bitter seedy cucumbers are gone. Also the F1 hybrids give astonishing yields and vigour, with types for greenhouses, cold-frames or outdoors.

All types require similar growing conditions, that is, very rich compost, copious supplies of both water and high nitrogenous liquid feeds when growing strongly, and they must be protected from cold and draughts. When planting it is strongly advisable to plant *on a slight mound*, and water around it, keeping the water away from the actual stem in the early days. Use water that has been warmed slightly to avoid a chill.

Varieties
All F1 Hybrids of course:
Pepinex, which is high-yielding with dark green fruits.
Danimas, which is small-fruited and very prolific.
Petita, another with mini-sized fruit, and a good taste and texture.
Paska, which can be grown outside in a sheltered spot or does well
　　　under a cloche.

COURGETTES

Courgettes belong to the same family as cucumbers, and so require similar treatment. Cloche protection in the early stages definitely gives them a flying start. Good varieties to try are: *Zuchini*, a reliable strain that should be cut young, and grows to approximately 6–8 inches long; or *Gold Rush*, which is golden-yellow in colour. Crop courgettes at least once a week to maintain a good supply; otherwise the fruit will become large, (they are of course a kind of marrow) and growth will virtually stop.

Cucumbers require cosseting—good rich compost and plenty of food and water.[‡]

PUMPKINS

Pumpkins are also members of the 'curcubit' family, and have become one of the latest enthusiast's plants, due to the huge sizes they can attain. The British record stands at way over 800 pounds, and, apart from pumpkin shows in towns and villages, most general shows now have a class for pumpkins, usually judged solely on weight.

The most popular variety by far is **Atlantic Giant**. If you're going to have a go, you'll need a fair amount of space, loads of water and feed, and you must restrict each plant to just one or two fruits if you want size. A cloche protection in the early season is very beneficial as a continuous growth pattern must be maintained. Take care when harvesting: they can be extremely heavy! Hand-pollination of the female flower is required, but it is quite simple. Take a fresh male flower—not necessarily from the same plant—remove the petals, and insert the pollen into the open flower of the female. The female flower is only 'receptive' for approximately twelve hours, so many keen growers cultivate additional plants in pots to ensure a supply of male flowers for this purpose.

MELONS

Admittedly, the melon is a fruit, but it does belong to the same curcubit family. I always feel they should be more widely grown, as the new strains are ideal—even in northern England—for cold-frame or cloche culture. They need similar treatment to all the other members of the curcubit family, which is rich soil with plenty of moisture, and they dislike cold damp conditions. Don't expect large crops, but you will certainly get sweet tender fruit if grown correctly. In a frame they require stopping after five pairs of leaves, then each lateral should be stopped at two pairs of leaves, as fruits form on the laterals. A high-nitrogen liquid feed will ensure rapid growth; switch to a high-potash feed after fruits have formed.

The 'Cantaloupe' strain are the most reliable and, as with pumpkins, hand-pollination ensures success. You can easily tell when they are ripe as a most delicious perfume is released. The variety that revolutionised melons for the amateur is still going strong and has stood the test of time. It is known as F1 hybrid **Sweetheart**, a reliable early variety that is small and sweet. **Ogden** is a mid-season variety with small to medium green fruit.

Results like this make all the effort and care worthwhile.†

LETTUCE

Lettuce is the widest grown of all the salad vegetables. The range is quite bewildering, and a matter of personal choice. As a general guide, it is true to say it is a very accommodating plant to grow, and you should aim to plant a small amount regularly to give continuity. With a cold-frame or greenhouse, lettuce can be produced 52 weeks of the year with careful selection of varieties. Winter lettuce cultivated in a greenhouse grows at a very much slower rate than summer varieties, so the most careful restricted watering is called for, with the removal of any plant debris. Multi-cell trays are ideal for raising young plants, as they ensure that minimum transplanting damage occurs.

Varieties

Butter-headed 'Iceberg' types and Cos are all available in profusion, including the newer red types which will give a splash of elegance to your salad bowl. As a sample of the many varieties available, below are a few of my own personal favourites, with which I don't think you'll be disappointed.

Butter-head Varieties. An early sort is **Fortune** with a good colour; and **All The Year Round** is as the name implies and very versatile.
Crisp Varieties. The standard variety is still **Iceberg**; **Webb's Wonderful** is large, green, and slow to bolt; **Picking Lettuce** form loose heads and the leaves can be picked as they are needed; **Lollo Rosso** is crisp, with a frilled edged in red; **Salad Bowl** is a non-hearting easy grower; **Cos** is a variety that I strongly suggest you try for a new lettuce experience; and not new but one that should be more widely grown is **Lobjoit's Green**, which is an upright self-blanching variety of a really deep green shade with taste in excess.

CHINESE LEAVES

Chinese leaves have advanced enormously in popularity over the last few years, as Chinese cooking has become more commonplace in British homes. They are mostly F1 Hybrids and can be used in salads or cooked as a winter vegetable. They are bred for our climate, so they are well worth a second glance.

Mixed lettuce in rows, and a Cos lettuce which has a wonderful flavour.‡

SWEETCORN

Sweetcorn, or 'corn on the cob' has been completely revamped by the growers in the last few years, with more reliable varieties becoming available. Careful sowing is essential in warm, moist compost and they should not be planted out until late May. To ensure pollination—sweetcorn is wind-pollinated—*plant in blocks not in rows*, with approximately 16–20 plants to a block. Timing of harvesting can present problems to the novice grower. To test for ripeness, carefully peel back the outer casing on a cob and press your thumbnail into the exposed kernels. If it is watery, then it is not ripe; if it is thick and creamy, then it is over-ripe; but if it is milk-coloured, it is perfect.

All varieties worth choosing are F1 hybrids. I suggest **Sundance**, which is very sweet and RHS-recommended. **Dickson** is quite tall at approximately six feet, but prolific and superb.

In concluding this chapter, may I again emphasise that gardening is a very a personal thing, and ever-changing due to the new varieties that are constantly appearing. However, I've tried to offer a broad spectrum of ideas and share with you some of the varieties that have delighted me in the hope that you'll derive the same pleasure.

Turnip Early Snowball seen here only twelve weeks after sowing.‡

A well-manicured lawn—the perfect foil for your plants.‡

Lawns

Those grand old trees with their splendid foliage and the thick green grass underneath is a sight to see — no one knows what grass is until they come to England!

Princess Victoria of Prussia
(writing to her mother, Dowager Empress Frederich of Prussia,
4th June, 1889).

NOTHING SETS OFF a flower border or shrubbery better than a lawn, whether it is twenty square yards or a thousand square yards. Well trimmed and with neat edges, a lawn is a perfect foil to your home and surroundings and speaks volumes for the skill of the gardener. Much expert advice has been written on the subject, so I shall restrict myself to comments of a general nature.

A generalisation that often holds true is that lawns are the most ill-treated, neglected and undernourished aspect of our gardens, and yet they seldom complain. They are used for all manner of games, sports and barbecues, they suffer drought, flooding and diseases, and usually receive scant attention. However, your lawn consists of literally thousands of plants and, with a little attention, will offer a lifetime's service.

PREPARATION

Preparation is, without doubt, the secret of success. Just as any good decorator will tell you, considerably more time is spent preparing than actually painting. The land should be deeply dug, and all weeds and stones should be removed. If the site is notoriously wet, you must consider incorporating either soakaways or land drains. The ground should be really well raked and firmed and a pre-seeding or planting fertiliser mixed into the top inch or so at 3–4 ounces per square yard. These fertilisers are available from a specialist garden centre, or you can make up a simple DIY one with: 1 part hoof and horn; 2 parts bonemeal; and 1 part sulphate of potash. All parts are by weight. Mix thoroughly and apply 5–7 days before laying turf or seeding.

TURF VERSUS SEED

The choice is entirely at your discretion, but a few pros and cons to help you to decide are listed below.

Turf

Advantages. It is quick: it can be walked on and look good in just a couple of weeks or so—'instant gardening'.

Disadvantages. It is very much more costly than seeding, and the quality of turf can vary considerably. I've seen excellent turf on sale and some that should have ended up in a court of law! My best advice on buying is to shop around. Visit neighbours who have bought turf and can recommend a supplier. Price is not always the best guide, but in general you get what you pay for.

Seeding

Advantages. It is cheaper than turf. Also, there is a wide choice of grades available, so a lawn can be sown to meet your specific needs.

Disadvantages. A seeded lawn takes longer to establish and the seed must be very carefully applied to ensure a uniform lawn. Also, changes in the weather can create problems at sowing time.

TURFING

Always start in one corner with a full turf and end the row with another one; any cut turfs should be fitted in the middle. Work from a board and butt turfs up closely by using a stout straight-edge and a mallet. Have a quantity of riddled soil and peat ready mixed to brush into the cracks between the turfs with a stiff broom. Although the lawn will look a dirty mess after this treatment, don't worry, because it assists the turfs in binding together, and it's amazing how quickly it greens up. Water it well if no rain falls over the 5–7 days after turfing.

SEEDING

Start by selecting the correct seed for your purpose. The finest for a superb lawn is a mixture that contains no ryegrass, as this will produce fine grasses of a real deep colour and create a dense sward. Obviously this is the 'Rolls Royce' of grass seed, and is unfortunately reflected in the price.

Mixtures with Ryegrass. These are cheaper and very hard-wearing, therefore ideal for a lawn on which children will be playing. These mixtures contain varying percentages of broad-bladed grasses. In all cases, sow at 1½ ounces per square yard on a still day; if showers are forecast, this is an added benefit. Many grass seed suppliers offer seed that has been treated with a bird repellent, which is a distinct help. After seeding, the area can profitably be covered with horticultural fleece, which will deter birds and create a micro-climate to assist germination. As with turf, water it with a sprinkler after 5–7 days if rain has not fallen.

LAWNMOWERS

There are two basic types of lawnmower, the cylindrical type or the rotary kind. Cylindrical lawnmowers give you the traditional stripes, and usually a better finish on quality lawns. The rotary types, particularly the 'hover' mowers afford a quicker cut and are adaptable to use on damp lawns. The power supply can be either manual, electric or petrol, depending on the depth of your pocket and the size of your lawn.

Whatever you decide, let your maxim be that the more frequently you mow, the better the finish. However, don't scalp your lawn. A half-inch minimum cut is ideal: you're not preparing a wicket for a five-day Test Match. For the first few cuts after laying, set your mower blades no lower than one inch, and ensure that the blades are kept sharp.

LAWN FEEDING AND CARE

I often wonder if the not-so-dedicated gardener realises how much grass is removed in a season of lawn mowing, and how little fertiliser so many lawns receive.

Feeding
Before we consider feeding our lawns, let us calculate their needs. Two distinct and different fertilisers are needed. Firstly a spring and summer feed is required to stimulate and green up our lawns in the period March to August. This should be of a high-nitrogen nature, and many proprietary feeds are available, in either powder or liquid form. Many incorporate a selective weedkiller, so we can kill two birds with one stone: sometimes a moss suppressant can also be included. A fertiliser applied in the autumn offers distinct benefits in toughening up the grass to withstand the rigors of winter. This should be *low* in nitrogen but *high* in phosphate and potash to be effective, and should be applied in October or November.

In a large lawn a specimen tree, here an acer, provides a focal point.

Moss

Various problems can beset our lawns, moss being a major culprit. I am often asked about remedies for moss, but we must beware of putting the cart before the horse: moss killers work, but we must treat the cause rather than the symptoms, otherwise it will return. The reason for moss is invariably bad or inadequate drainage, and can be rectified by a treatment of scarifying and spiking—or, even better, use a hollow-tined fork that extracts cores from your lawn. This should be carried out during a dry spell in late October or November and followed by an autumn lawn dressing. I promise you your lawn will get away to a flying start the following spring.

Edging

To give any lawn a well-manicured appearance, edging is essential. This can be done either manually with edging shears, or much more quickly and easily by either an attachment to fit your mower or a strimmer fitted with a swivel head.

Hollows

In existing old lawns, hollows can often be a problem. A simple solution is to mark out over the offending hollow a letter 'H' using an edging iron or straight-bladed spade. Insert the spade carefully to a depth of at least three inches and then peel back the turf. Have a prepared mix of three parts riddled soil, one part peat, and one part silver sand, and insert this into the hollow portion. Replace the turf and brush a little of the mixture into the cracks.

Broken Edges

Similarly, if you have a broken lawn edge, cut out the offending turf as a square, turn it through 180 degrees and replace it so that the damaged part is now in the lawn area proper. The bare spot will soon grow in, or if it doesn't you can use a 'lawn patch', which are readily available. Or you can grow your own lawn patches—see 'Useful Tips' chapter.

Specimen Trees

I always feel use should be made of a specimen tree as a focal point or centrepiece of a lawn. It draws one's eye and lends character to the lawn. The choice is wide: magnolia, flowering cherry, or, for the small lawn, flowering almond with its narrow width and columnar shape are all ideal. And of course for the pocket-handkerchief-sized lawn, what better than a small standard 'Kilmarnock Willow'? The choice is yours, but do think of the ultimate height and girth whatever you choose.

I will conclude this brief discourse on lawns with the following two formulations which I developed some time ago, they are easily made up and have proved very successful. All the ingredients are readily available from a good garden store.

Autumn Lawn Tonic

In spring it is essential to feed your lawn, and the best way to do this is the 'weed and feed' method. However, it's just as important to give your lawn an autumn tonic to toughen up the grass and roots for the winter.

First prepare the lawn with a scarifier, hollow-tined fork or lawn rake to aerate and remove any debris. Then make up the feed, as follows (parts are by weight).

- 1 part sulphate of ammonia
- 2 parts bonemeal
- 4 parts sulphate of potash

Mix thoroughly and apply at two ounces per square yard maximum. A handy tip that I mentioned earlier is to measure the first two ounces in a plastic cup and mark the level with a pen. Then all you need to do is fill up to the mark for each square yard. The simplest way to mark out your square yard is to use four three-foot canes, which are readily available at any garden store or centre. Place them on the lawn to make a square in one corner. Feed within the area marked out by the canes and then move three of the canes to make the next square, working your way across the lawn making sure that each square yard has an *equal* distribution of the feed. It's very important that you *don't* cover any area twice! If it doesn't rain within seven days after feeding, water the lawn.

Using this tonic will give you the basis for an excellent lawn the following summer.

SPRING AND SUMMER LAWN FERTILISER WITH MOSS SUPPRESSANT

A good home-made feed can be made as follows (all parts are by weight).

- 4 parts sulphate of ammonia
- 1 part bonemeal
- 2 parts sulphate of potash
- 1 part sulphate of iron (to suppress moss formation)

Add half the weight of the total ingredients listed above in fine horticultural sand (not builders' sand). For example, if one part in the above weighs one pound, then the total ingredients will weigh eight pounds. Therefore, four pounds of sand is required. Mix it in thoroughly and apply at two ounces per square yard maximum.

As with the autumn lawn tonic you *must* apply the mixture evenly, and *don't* cover the same area twice. Again, if there's no rain within seven days after applying the feed, water the lawn. To keep your lawn green and attractive, it is necessary to repeat the treatment at least once more in high summer.

A lawn with formal beds.

A show winning collection of vegetables.

Growing for Showing

The true gardener, like a true artist, is never satisfied.

H.E. Bates

I HAVE BEEN ASKED countless times what is the point of showing. The most frequent comment I've heard is: 'I'm not interested in showing; I'm just producing good results for my own pleasure', I have no quarrel with this attitude, but pause for a moment and consider a few salient points. First and foremost, growing for showing is good fun. Secondly, on a more serious note, it's amazing that wherever one goes, whether it's a local village show or a major county or national show, the same varieties of exhibit crop up with unfailing regularity. Ask yourself why. The simple reason is that the consistently successful variety has an inherent quality that makes it stand out above the rest, so surely that is the one we should be growing.

Shows are of course the shop window for our many and varied societies and clubs, which offer entertainment, comradeship and knowledge to all—long may they continue. The general gardener can learn so much from the exhibitor, and at the same time is given a yardstick by which to judge his own efforts. The visitor to today's show may become tomorrow's national champion.

Planning ahead is so vital to achieve success. Dedication and single-mindedness are very much the watchwords—not that it should become a drudge or a chore: gardening is a fun subject! The vast majority of show organisers do their best to co-operate with growers by fixing show dates very early; in fact the norm is to announce dates a year in advance at the actual show. Although gardening is not an exact science, there are six golden rules that can be summed up as follows:

1. Grow the right variety or strain.
2. Keep good records of sowing dates, feeding regime, maturing dates, and results.
3. Remember attention to detail and regular routine cultivation is the path to success.

4. The national champions in most classes restrict their growing to a very limited range of crops; in other words, they specialise. Ask yourself if this is for you.

5. Allow plenty of time when showing to cut, transport and stage your exhibits. It's so sad to see a year's effort spoilt by rushing the final hurdle.

6. Last, but by no means least, be a 'good loser'. We can't all take the red card, and there is always another year.

To elaborate on these 'rules' of mine, I will make the following points.

VARIETY OR STRAIN

These are constantly changing. A glance at old show results and records proves that new and better varieties are in many cases replacing the winners of yesteryear. Stock selection of existing strains is essential: any chrysanthemum grower worth his salt will tell you that when storing his 'stools' over winter for next season's cuttings, he rogues out any that have not given perfect results and only retains the show-winners. While the plants are still flowering, it is a handy tip to tie a piece of coloured wool round the bottom of the stems of the best plants, then you can discard all the others. Similarly, the onion and leek wizards always retain the prize winners for re-seeding and hope that the progeny from these will be on the winning rostrum in two years' time. An element of luck must play a part, of course, but the right variety and strain must be the starting point. You can't make a silk purse out of a sow's ear.

RECORDS

The memory can play tricks so it is important to keep a record of all dates: sowing, planting, feeding and spraying. An accurate knowledge of the timespan of these activities for each variety is essential, and the dates can in future years be amended as we learn by experience. It makes for success to start each growing season with a firm plan based on past successes, or, more usually, failures. While perfection is virtually impossible, we can all improve our results.

ATTENTION TO DETAIL

The only addition I would make to my suggested Rule 3 is the important point of holidays. Most crops we grow for showing have either a dormant season or, at the very least, periods when very little

routine work is required so holidays can be fitted in easily. After all, even the obsessive gardener needs a break.

SPECIALISATION

Most exhibitors, and I'm no exception, try to grow too many crops and so miss out on the top awards—but we do have fun! The specialists are invariably gardeners who have run the whole gamut of local showing and developed a special love of one or two crops, usually because they've built up a good knowledge and expertise of them. Having acquired this single-mindedness they go from strength to strength, and become the people responsible for the 800lb-plus pumpkins and 12lb-plus onions, to name but two.

TRANSPORTING AND STAGING

What you are taking and how far you are travelling dictates the packing and transporting of your exhibits. I know of one celebrated Lancashire fuchsia exhibitor who actually hired a furniture van to transport his standard fuchsias and hanging baskets to a major show. Such enterprise deserves success, and he usually achieves it. The most important point, as always, is to plan ahead. You'll find most show-growers have a checklist of what they need and a box or case to keep it all in. The usual contents include: marker pen, card, name tags, dusters, paper clips, sticky tape, camel hair brushes, sponge, tweezers, and, most importantly, a show schedule.

Spare exhibits are a must. Imagine travelling a hundred miles with a superb set of five chrysanthemums to find one is marked or damaged on arrival—the thought makes the blood run cold. Always arrive early at the show and try to find a quiet corner where you can happily set up your exhibits. If you're a new exhibitor, do try to watch some of the old hands: you'll learn a lot and usually receive any help or advice you need. The veterans of the show world have their own collection of show aids, such as back-boards for vegetable collections, rose boxes, onion stands, and special clips to hold name cards. After all, in a close-run competition the best-staged exhibit— all other points being equal—usually gets the nod.

The most unwanted mark on an exhibit after judging are the letters 'N.A.S.'. This stands for 'not as schedule', denoting that the rules or specifications have been broken. On many occasions when judging, I've found an extra pod on a plate of twelve pods of peas, or, for example, on a class that calls for 'three onions, grown from seed, as grown' the roots have been trimmed to the plate, the tops removed and outer skins peeled off.

World record onion September 1995 weight 15lb 9½ oz—Mel Ednie at Harrogate.•

The '95 champion pumpkin—weight 599½ lbs.•

No judge worth his salt takes any pleasure from disqualifying an entry. After all, his job should be to increase the number of competitors not disillusion them, but it is a narrow path that judges tread. Common sense should prevail. In the first example with the plate of peas, my approach is to mention to the curator accompanying the judge that I'll go and judge another class and perhaps he would care to take a look at the plate of peas in question in my temporary absence. On my return one hopes that the plate now contains the correct number. With regard to the onions, regrettably this would have to be a case of 'N.A.S.'.

Planning ahead for shows starts after the last show of any year, when one formulates one's plans for the next season, and for the favoured few the challenge of defending one's crown. But even the cutting of flowers and preparing of veg calls for a plan of action.

Flowers are best cut early in the morning before the heat rises, and placed in deep containers of water: it's worth remembering what a drop of liquid feed added to the water will do. All large thick-stemmed flowers—gladioli are a perfect example—should be cut at an angle of 45°. This exposes the maximum amount of stem tissue to take up water, and every 24 hours a thin sliver should again be removed, plunging your hands and scissors into the container rather than removing the stem . Dahlias have a hollow stem and an embolism or 'air lock' can easily occur. More than once in massed dahlia classes you'll see an odd bloom looking like a rag due to this. The rule with dahlias is to take water to your dahlias, not your dahlias to water. In other words, place containers of water at your dahlia beds and, immediately after cutting, plunge the stems into water. This is simple but essential.

Root vegetables are usually cleaned by using a soft sponge and plenty of water; a mixture of milk and water definitely improves potatoes. Peas should be picked early in the morning with the bloom still on them and cut with a stalk or handle approximately half an inch long. Try not to handle the pods, and have trays lined with soft material to hand to lay them in. A strong light—either sunlight or a torch—will show up any missing peas in the pods. Runner beans should be also cut with a stalk. Take a flat board, lay damp cloths on top, then the beans and then more damp cloth on top, followed by another board. This will help to flatten or 'iron' the beans overnight. These are all legal tricks of the trade.

Check the schedule, then check it again. Remember each show has its own idiosyncracies. Different conditions are often required for vegetables; for example, onions may be required to be dressed or 'as grown'. 'As grown' means exactly that, although it is not expected that onions and potatoes will be dumped on the tables heavy with

The author exhibiting gladioli at The Sheffield Show.

clods of earth. They should just be washed and dried but with the roots and tops still intact. When veg are to be shown 'dressed', this usually means tops and roots neatly trimmed and loose skin removed. Care should be taken if an exact length of root or top is stipulated. This is often the case with onions, beetroot and leeks, and must be strictly adhered to.

TYPES OF SHOWS

While, regrettably, some shows have declined in the last decade, other sections and classes are increasing. The most popular new class that has swept the country and invariably attracts a very high entry is one named 'Floraveg'. This consists of one flower and one vegetable shown together, each is individually judged and scored out of a total of ten points in one-quarter increments. The scores are shown and totalled on each exhibit—it promotes considerable interest amongst visitors. More often than not the best flower and best vegetable do not win as they are not together. This class was originated at small society shows to encourage all members to enter and has progressed from there. Anyone interested in promoting a show or competition could do no better than try this class: it's a proven winner and popular with most.

The purists often say this is not real top competition, but I would not subscribe to this view. Anything that increases entries and is a real attraction should not be decried. It's also a great starting point for any new member of the gardening fraternity to test the water and delve into showing. Another fairly new class is 'giant pumpkins'. These are becoming universally popular, and like onions, weights continue to rise. The world record currently stands at well over 800 pounds. They may be ugly, but they draw the crowds. Winning heavyweights are all bred from the variety *Atlantic Giant*, but re-selected and re-selected. They take up lots of space, thriving on extensive feeding and watering, the trick being to keep them growing for as long as possible.

The number of daffodil shows is also on the increase, and they are now becoming very popular, and rightly so. Daffs are becoming bigger and better thanks to the small dedicated band of daff breeders and they fill a special niche in the garden calendar. Taking place early in the year (March and April), daffodil shows are a great springboard for the whole season ahead and fit in well in most gardeners' years. They can be grown outdoors in beds or potted and flowered in greenhouses or polythene tunnels. A visit to a daffodil show can be a real eye-opener to the uninitiated: hundreds of blooms, from white to pink, orange and red, single- and multi-headed,

Chrysanthemums fit for the show.‡

many with an exquisite perfume, all under one roof—quite a spectacle. Many Midland and Northern licensed premises now run 'mini' daffodil and flower shows and they are proving an alternative attraction to pub quizzes.

BE A GOOD LOSER

Although I cannot claim impartiality in my opinion, I believe that judges are a much-maligned and criticised section of society. Strict rules and guidelines are laid down by all the main ruling bodies and are adhered to, but of course judges are human and mistakes can happen. Also when visiting a show, always remember exhibits are judged as seen at the time of judging. The reason I make this point is that at major shows which run for two or three days, exhibits such as roses, sweet peas and dahlias can look very different on the last day, particularly if held in a marquee on hot summer days.

Most judges are always pleased to answer questions and I believe judges' comments on entries are always welcome and usually informative to the general public. *National Vegetable Society* scorecards on vegetable collections are always a great source of interest and do help to remove some of the mystique of judging.

GROWING

The choice of variety is by far the first priority in show growing. Techniques also vary: specialist growers use very sophisticated equipment such as supplementary lighting in greenhouses for early growth on leeks and onions, coupled with automatic heating, ventilation and irrigation. The élite top growers plant all leeks and onions under polythene tunnels or structures and monitor each stage of growth very carefully. The long parsnips and carrots are usually grown in drums of sand with boreholes made with a boring bar, each hole filled with a carefully-prepared growing mix. Two or three seeds are sown at each station, covered with a mini-cloche or jam jar to create a micro-climate and thinned to one per station. To harvest, the drums are tipped on their sides and the crops extracted with great care to ensure the long tap root is intact. This is all a far cry from growing for the table in the open garden.

The only slight misgiving I have on all the modern methods employed for show growing is that to compete on a level with the show-winners, one must have a rather deep pocket to purchase all the necessary equipment.

JUDGING

If you can be second — and with the Judge agree,
You're an honest gardener — and a better man than me.

R.I.J.

We all view our own exhibits with a certain partiality, but one can learn so much by studying the winning entries. Firstly, of course, you should note what variety has been grown, and secondly pay attention to the staging and overall impact. I believe that societies and judges should do everything they can to explain by means of cards, written comments and guidelines in schedules exactly what constitutes a winning entry, and thus take some of the mystique out of exhibiting. The National Vegetable Society have gone a long way down this route with their points system and scorecards for collection of vegetables. It makes very interesting reading.

The winning entry in many classes often picks itself, standing out head and shoulders above the rest, but deciding the minor places is the one that usually gives me the biggest problem when judging. I regret to say that all too frequently a good entry is spoilt due to the name of the variety being written on a tatty bit of paper or piece torn from a cigarette packet and written with a blunt pencil, obviously added as an afterthought.

Everything we can do in preparation before we leave home is a bonus, and writing the name cards (watch your spelling) should be one of them. At many shows a section is devoted to floral art, and I always think that the comments written on each entry by the judge are of interest both to the general public and the entrant. The judges in the horticultural sections could do well to take note and follow suit. I realise that this would be time-consuming, but anything to both help the entrants and be of interest to visitors can do nothing but good; after all, the more we can increase the appeal of the shows the more they will prosper. More and younger exhibitors are badly needed in certain shows and sections to ensure progress. May I make an appeal for more helpers and assistance at your societies' shows: there is always a small nucleus of over-worked committee members who would be glad of a little support.

Exhibiting is a time-consuming occupation, and can be rather expensive if one does not exercise caution. However, I know of nothing more rewarding, and it is the basis of many friendships built on seasons of mutual respect, with help and advice always freely given. Every year exhibitors talk of cutting down on the number of entries or shows they plan to subscribe to, but once the crops start to mature, the adrenalin starts to flow and off we go again.

Useful Tips

ALL SO-CALLED GARDENING PUNDITS have over the years collected a wealth of gardening tips from many sources, and I am no exception. This section contains some of my tried and tested gardening hints, and I trust you will find some old ones you had forgotten and some new ones to try. Hopefully you will find them both cost- and time-saving. They are not in any particular order of importance or value, but they should all make your life just that little bit easier.

Rhubarb

Rhubarb Ted

I knew a funny little man,
His name was Rhubarb Ted,
They called him that because he wore,
Rhubarb on his head.
I'd grown so used to this strange sight,
The cause I did not seek,
But then one day to my surprise,
I saw he wore a leek.
I asked him if he'd please explain,
And let me know the reason,
He said 'I'm wearing leek because,
Rhubarb's out of season'!

Anne O'Connor

We all know how to produce succulent early sticks: usually a bucket, without a bottom, or a box, is placed over a clump in early February to hasten growth, and of course old manure or garden compost is piled on to increase the warmth. Do this, but at the same time cover the *outside* of your box or bucket with manure or compost. This further increases the warmth and speeds up the whole process quite dramatically.

Long Leeks

I must of course follow the rhubarb with a tip on the blanching of long leeks. It's amazing how much free material is wasted on

The author preparing flowers for showing. The bags protect the flower heads from pests and provide a mini-greenhouse effect. You will note that the bags are dated and will be removed 28–32 days later to reveal 'perfect' blooms.*

building sites and builders' yards. Offcuts of plastic downpipes are often lying around, and these do a splendid job of blanching leeks. (Do, however, ask before you take.) Any bore size will do: a one-inch diameter in the young stages of growth and up to a four-inch diameter are all very useful. If ends are jagged, they are easily cut with a fine-toothed hacksaw. Lengths can be of varying size to suit your plants. With the larger diameters, it helps to place riddled soil or peat down the pipe after covering the leeks, as it excludes the light and also makes for a longer length of blanch. An added bonus is that liquid feed can, with great benefit, be applied down the pipes to promote exhibition specimens.

Yellow Sticky Glue Traps

These are now extremely popular in many amateur greenhouses. They are spin-offs from the professional growers, who have been using them for many years. They not only catch many 'baddies', but also enable you to monitor the pests you are harbouring—simply check your traps after a week or so to see what you have caught. They originated in Germany, where it was found that a bright yellow colour was by far the most effective.

Without wishing to deprive retail outlets of business, a very simple and renewable one can quite easily be made. Take a piece of hardboard or thick card approximately six inches by three inches. About an inch in from one of the 3-inch sides, drill a small hole (this is for inserting the string to suspend the trap). Paint both sides with the brightest yellow gloss paint you can find. After it dries, smear both sides of your trap with either clear Vaseline or light-coloured grease. Hang it in your greenhouse and watch the results. The further advantage of these DIY traps is that when they are well covered by pests they can be cleaned with hot soapy water, dried, re-greased and returned to their original place in the greenhouse.

Row or Bed Markers

A simple and effective marker can be made by using either a lath of thin wood or a new rigidly-straight garden cane. (The depth of winter is a good time to prepare this type of aid.) Mark out either with bright paint or coloured electrician's tape various measurements in various increments, using imperial or metric, depending on your preference. This saves carrying a rule or tape around the garden when planting or preparing beds. You can also use your hand-trowel or fork if you measure both the blade and the overall length and remember it. This is very helpful when planting out bedding plants and vegetables.

Mini Cloches

Lemonade and cola is now readily available in one- and two-litre round plastic bottles—the larger the better for our purpose. Using a fine-toothed hacksaw, cut the empty bottles approximately 6–9 inches from the top (keep the screw cap). Placed over young plants and seedlings, they create an excellent micro-climate to promote growth and deter pests. On cold nights, the screw cap can be replaced as a frost deterrent, then taken off for ventilation as the temperature rises. They are a great help over lettuce seedlings and early radish, and have the added safety factor of being plastic. They can be securely staked with a hoop made from a free-of-charge wire coat hanger from your local dry cleaners.

Egg Boxes

The six- and twelve-partition versions make ideal trays for 'chitting' your seed potatoes on a light kitchen window sill in February.

Plant Labels

These have increased in price every time I buy some. A simple supply can be made by cutting up old washing-up liquid bottles and making the usual-size plant labels. Place them in very hot water for ten minutes then put them under a weight—a brick wrapped in newspaper is ideal—overnight to flatten them.

Tubs, Urns and Patio Planters

I invariably find that the cheaper end of the range either have inadequate drainage holes or even none. This of course can lead to disease due to stagnation when planted up. The easy way of inserting more holes is with a really hot poker to burn through the container. Do this outdoors, however, as the fumes can be both unpleasant and toxic.

Compost Heaps

The benefits of compost heaps need no further elaboration from me. However, don't forget two valuable ingredients: eggshells, a prime source of calcium, and teabags, which are totally organic, so don't waste them.

Wire Coat-Hangers

With grateful thanks to the dry-cleaners, wire coat-hangers have a multitude of uses, due to their smoothness and versatility, as plant ties and straining ties when used in conjunction with elastic bands.

Seed Containers

A plastic box, with a lid, is ideal for storing seeds and can be considerably improved by making a quantity of card dividers. These can be identified or numbered by weeks so that seeds can be inserted in order, ensuring that sowing dates are not missed. As we know, sowing dates can be critical.

Tray and Pot Levellers

I have a selection of home-made levellers, and in spring they are used regularly. They can be made quite simply in either wood or thin sheet metal with a handle attached made from an old broom shaft. I have two sizes of round ones, four and six inches in diameter, and rectangular ones to level both half and full seed tray sizes. Apart from neatness, they ensure even germination of seeds.

Car Boot Kit

As standard equipment in a car boot, I believe any self-respecting keen gardener will carry empty compost or fertiliser bags and a trowel or small spade. It's amazing what you can find deposited on verges and roadsides by horses, or in autumn you can collect fresh leaves for leaf-mould—beech and oak are best if you have the choice.

Charcoal

Wood ash is a natural and organic source of potash (as explained in the fertiliser section), but also part-burnt wood produces charcoal, which is a 'sweetener' for home-made bulb fibre. While discussing bulb fibres, when next you treat yourself to half a dozen oysters, wash the shells very thoroughly to remove all traces of the sea, dry in an oven, then break them up to fine fragments. Four ounces of oyster shell fragments, plus four ounces of home-made charcoal, plus two ounces of superphosphate all thoroughly mixed into a two-gallon bucket of granulated sphagnum peat makes a great DIY bulb fibre.

Rainwater Butts

In these days of water meters and water conservation, we are all doing our own bit in saving water by the use of storage tubs. However, even with a good-fitting lid, algae can form very quickly, adding a teaspoonful of potassium permanganate crystals every week or so works wonders.

Replacement Windows

I am often offered old windows by listeners who are having double-glazed units fitted. Should these come your way, do avail yourself of them. They make excellent temporary or permanent garden frames. Used in conjunction with a few dozen bricks a temporary frame can be fashioned in minutes, or a permanent one constructed by using mortar to secure the brickwork.

Feet for Window Boxes, Tubs and Urns
A circulation of air under and around these kinds of containers is very beneficial and creates the right atmosphere. The screw lids from coffee jars, which are usually matt brown in colour, make ideal feet for them, being of a wide diameter but a shallow height.

When It Snows
I know only too well the damage that snow can do to our gardens and plants. Snow is incredibly heavy, and you should make every effort to knock snow from trees, bushes and shrubs, unless it is frozen. However, snow on a garden frame acts as an insulation and should be left to melt in its own good time. On a greenhouse roof this should be carefully taken off: I've seen so many greenhouse roofs collapse under the sheer weight. One of the best—and safest methods—is to increase the temperature in your greenhouse to precipitate a thaw. I appreciate that heat is expensive, but nothing compared to a new roof!

Horticultural Fleece
One of the greatest new products to come our way, horticultural fleece is another spin-off from the commercial growers. Its uses for covering early crops, as a pest deterrent and to bring crops forward is widely publicised, but I have a further suggestion, which is widely practised in the USA and on golf courses. When laying new seed lawns or carrying out lawn repair work where grass seed is being used, create a micro-climate with horticultural fleece. It speeds up germination, and acts as a bird deterrent. Horticultural fleece really accelerates the whole process and creates a very quick and successful lawn without tears.

Late spring frosts can really be a problem to gardeners, who at that time of year usually have greenhouses and frames bulging with plants. Keep a spare roll of fleece, or odd pieces that you've saved from previous use, ready to drape over your cuttings and seedlings. If frost threatens, bring out the fleece. Even a single thickness will give several degrees of frost protection, and being as light as gossamer, it can be laid directly on your seedlings without doing any damage.

Containers can look beautiful—keep a circulation of air under them for best results.

Bonus Vegetables

Two simple tried and tested ideas are as follows. All you need for success is a reasonably good autumn and a little knowhow.

Summer Cabbages
When these mature, don't dig them up, but cut them off with secateurs approximately two inches above ground level. Score a cross approximately a quarter-inch deep in the stump, remove any weeds and apply a light dusting of general fertiliser. From the segments on the stump fresh mini-cabbages will be produced, along the lines of spring cabbage, to give a supply of fresh greens in October.

Broad Beans
Similarly, a second crop of fresh beans can be produced, although they will not be as prolific as your first crop. After cropping, which is usually in early July, cut down the main stem leaving approximately a two-inch stump. As with the summer cabbage mentioned above, remove any weeds, stir up the soil lightly and apply a dressing of general fertiliser. With only average conditions, a further feast of tender beans will be yours in the autumn.

Old Growbag Compost

At the last count, the sale of growbags in the UK had passed the two million mark. This represents quite a tonnage of organic humus, and I wonder what percentage is wasted after the original crop of tomatoes and cucumbers have been harvested. While a second crop of these vegetables is not a viable proposition, a winter secondary crop of lettuce or radish is possible by removing all the debris, stirring up the compost and adding six ounces of general fertiliser, well mixed in. Alternatively, the spent compost makes a grand mulch around shrubs and climbers, acting as a water retainer and also as a weed suppressant. The main point is: don't waste it—it's natural, it's humus, it's soil conditioner, and it's yours.

Frost Protection for Tubs, Urns and Containers
We are all aware of the importance of giving some form of protection to our more tender plants grown in containers by mulching the root area with a carpet of compost, old manure or bark chippings and draping fleece over the stems and branches—but that really is only half the battle. Many plants die due to frost penetrating the container walls and freezing the root ball solid. A worthwhile tip is to wrap bubble plastic around the outside of each tub and secure

Give seed potatoes a spray of fertiliser to produce a good crop. Here Pentland Javelin.‡

with twine or plastic wire. It may not look very elegant, but it can save many a precious plant in a hard winter.

Not-So-Obvious Uses for Liquid Fertiliser

Assisting Cuttings
We all know that various soft-wood cuttings—fuchsias are a prime example—can be readily rooted in a glass of water. However, by adding just a few drops of a balanced liquid feed to the water, a much stronger and more vigorous root system is produced, so that your cuttings get a flying start.

'Chitting' or Sprouting Seed Potatoes
A spray of a weak balanced liquid fertiliser, at room temperature, on your seed potatoes when set up in boxes to sprout will encourage the emerging shoots to be much stronger and more vigorous, thus giving the crop a great boost.

Hyacinths
Over the years, hyacinths have generated more questions and disappointments than most other potted bulbs, so I shall offer a few suggestions. The first criterion for a Christmas or 'forced' bloom is to ensure that the bulbs have had the full and correct 'pre-cooling' or 'preparing'. The process then falls into three stages:

1. The cold plunge
2. The introduction of light
3. The final stage: blooming

Cold Plunge
This means that the bulb, after potting, remains in a cool environment (7° Celsius maximum), without light, for approximately ten weeks. This is the vital stage when a solid root mass is formed. A dry cellar or cold store shed where light can be excluded is ideal.

However, a Victorian method is probably still the best. Thoroughly water the container after planting your hyacinths, then wrap the bowl in several layers of newspaper. Then in a spare spot in your garden dig a hole approximately a foot deep and place your bowls of hyacinths in the bottom. Cover it with bracken or straw then replace the topsoil. Leave them for approximately ten weeks, then dig them up, remove the newspaper and clean the outside of the bowls. The bulbs should have formed lots of roots and shoots approximately two inches high, which will be white of course, as light could not reach them and therefore photosynthesis could not take place.

Introducing Light

The second stage is to give them light to green up the leaves but *not warmth*. Too much warmth at this stage is one of the main causes of aborted or leggy flowers. If potted in late August, they should be ready for bringing into the light around the first week of November. A well-ventilated cold-frame or a shelf in a cold greenhouse is perfect for them.

Third and Final Stage

When the flower spikes are quite pronounced, your bowl can then take its place with pride in your lounge.

A further tip is when colour is evident in the flower, sprinkle a little grass seed on the compost: it will make a delightful green carpet. This is much more aesthetically pleasing than the dark shade of bulb fibre.

Staking Hyacinth Blooms

We have all experienced the difficulty of staking the heavy blooms and stems, particularly when grown in a bulb-fibre. I always compare it to trying to plant canes in a bag of marshmallows! All is not lost, however, as there is a simple trick, which is to take a short piece of the green slender hardwood canes available everywhere, sharpen one end to a point and plunge this into the shoulder of the bulb itself. You won't kill the bulb, and it then becomes a simple matter to tie the bloom.

Lawn Patches

With the best will in the world, accidents will happen and often these will result in bare patches on your lawn or badly-damaged lawn edges. It's a simple matter to make your own repair kit or patches by sowing grass seed in a one-inch depth of compost in both full-size and half-size seed trays. Placed in a cold-frame or greenhouse you will have perfect patches in four weeks or less.

Hanging Baskets

Hanging baskets are one of the delights of gardening, and a focal point of our front porches. I always maintain that first impressions are so important, and what is more welcoming than the sight of a well-filled hanging basket as one approaches a home for the first time? One of the most important tasks is the regular watering of the baskets, and this can be quite a chore. Admittedly, the water-retaining granules do a first-class job, and we can now buy a block and tackle arrangement to lower the basket to make watering easier; or use a 'pump' can with an extended feeding lance to save the risk of climbing up to water them.

However, I'd like to describe a simple 'fun' method to you: one, incidentally, guaranteed to keep youngsters amused if you offer a simple prize or bribe. In high summer, when the weather's hot, line up your youngsters and give each an even number of ice cubes from the freezer. They gently throw these up aiming to land them in the basket. The one with most cubes in the basket wins.

Apart from keeping the baskets watered, the melting ice also cools the plants in the heat of summer, and the idea can be taken a step further by adding some weak liquid feed when making the ice cubes: the nutrient supply is more prolonged when applied in the form of ice cubes. However, remember not to use them in your gin and tonic!

Anemones

The spring flowers *St Brigid* and *Decaen* anemones always have a wide appeal as cut flowers with their wide colour range. All anemones, whatever the type, are grown from dehydrated corms, and people often inform me that they have failed to grow. The secret is to soak them overnight in plain water. This plumps them up and assists enormously in breaking their dormancy. Don't be concerned about which way up to plant them: they don't have a top or bottom.

White Fly Menace

In a greenhouse, tomatoes, peppers and fuchsias suffer badly with infestation of white fly. One means of depleting their number, apart from yellow glue traps and insecticides, is with a vacuum cleaner with a long open flexible pipe. Tap your plants and then literally suck the insects up. It sounds fiendish, but any weapon against white fly can't be ignored.

Slugs

Slugs are a constant problem for gardeners, particularly on heavy land or during wet spells. One of the easiest and most environmentally-sound cures is to fill a shallow dish (a margarine carton is ideal) with beer, sink it in a border where slugs are active, and partly cover it with a flat stone. Slugs will be attracted by the smell, and, hey presto, they die a happy death.

Plastic Guttering

Plastic guttering is now used extensively, and many odd pieces can be acquired if one asks around. They can be put to very good use in a greenhouse for raising various crops. My particular suggestion is for that luxury veg crop, garden peas. We all have experienced the ravages of birds and slugs on emerging pea seedlings. Using short lengths of the guttering, somewhere between one and three feet long, half-filling them with a light friable compost, and sowing peas half an inch deep every two inches, a germination rate can be achieved of nearly 100%. Have your rows prepared by taking out a shallow trench roughly the depth of your guttering. When your seedlings have achieved about three inches of growth, water them well and gently slide the whole lot—peas and compost—into their awaiting trench. The result is no root or bird damage and a flying start for your crop.

Growbags

I have already discussed these earlier, but other uses can be made of them. One particular tip of mine is to cut a bag in half, and, ensuring each half has an equal share of the contents, stand them on end to make ideal deep containers. Their uses can be many, both in a greenhouse and outdoors. Crops that revel in a deep root-run are potato, celery, carrots and parsnips. Don't forget that, after cropping, the exhausted compost can be used around your shrubs as a valuable mulch.

Universal Measuring Cup

Drinks-dispensing machines are ubiquitous and accessible, many of which dispense a white plastic cup. A very useful and time-saving measuring device can be made from one of these and two different coloured indelible marker pens. Carefully measure out, in either fluid ounces or millilitres, liquid fertilisers in various increments. Pour each into your cup and draw a clear line against the height of the liquid. Carry out the same exercise with your dry powdered or granular fertilisers using the other coloured marker pen and make your graduated scale on the other side of the cup. Don't use this measure for weedkillers or insecticides, but make a separate measuring cup for these and wash it out thoroughly after use. You'll wonder how you managed without these home-made measures when you put them into use.

Coffee Jar Propagators

I have already extolled the virtues of the screw-top lids of coffee jars as mini-feet under tubs and window boxes. The whole jar can also serve as a first-class free-of-charge mini-propagator when used as follows.

Take a large clear coffee jar or similar with parallel sides and a screw-top—the bigger the jar the better. Wash it out thoroughly and remove any labels. Place the lid, open side up, on a flat surface and find a small plant pot that fits easily into it. Fill your plant pot with a suitable rooting compost and insert one or more soft wood cuttings. Fuchsias are easy to root this way, but any soft wood cuttings will be fine. Water it well, then invert the jar and screw it down into the lid. Leave it for three weeks; there is no need to water it as there will be plenty of humidity in the enclosed micro-climate you have created. After three weeks you'll find your cuttings are rooted and ready for potting on. Dipping the end of the cuttings in a rooting hormone powder or liquid will aid faster rooting.

Safety First

Like most gardeners, I use odd sheets of old glass, cut to size, to cover my seed trays to assist germination in my propagators, and on the open staging. If you are like me, you will find that your fingers and the glass are anything but compatible. A helpful tip is to cover all the edges of your pieces of glass with sticky tape, either clear or insulating. This stiffens the glass and prevents minor cuts from the sharp edges. I also make a large cross with the tape on each piece of glass, as this makes them much more visible, again reducing the risk of accidents.

Brassica Collars

One of the main problems of brassica growing is the evil cabbage root fly, or rather its grub, which tunnels down and devours the root. A good tip for halting its progress is to make simple collars to encircle the plant stems when planting out. Take some carpet underfelt or thin pieces of soft carpet, and cut a circle approximately three inches in diameter. Punch a quarter-inch hole in the centre, then cut from outer edge to this hole. The collar can then be slipped neatly round the stem—again, simple but effective.

Pansies

Aquilegia

Modern Science and Technology

GARDENING HAS NEVER BEEN, and never will be, an exact science, but when I look back I marvel at the improvements and developments that have taken place.

It has often been said about farming that when the horses left the land, so did many of the workers. Because of the tractor and mechanisation in general, labour has declined drastically. The same trend has occurred in the horticultural industry. As gardeners we can take advantage of modern advances to produce bigger and better crops, and—perhaps more importantly—experience increased leisure time to enjoy the fruits of our efforts.

PROPAGATORS

In my early years on an allotment, our achievements were remarkable considering the crude methods employed. I remember my first so-called 'propagator', which comprised an open bench, on which I placed a corrugated sheet of metal (from an old air-raid shelter), laid a layer of builders' sand on it, and on top of that an old wooden box with the bottom removed. Into this went my pots and boxes of seeds and cuttings and finally an old sheet of glass was placed on top. The source of heat was a small paraffin heater under the open bench, and a length of hessian (from an old potato sack) nailed across the front to keep the heat in. It was crude, but effective. Many's the time I dashed over to the allotment on a winter night with a gallon of paraffin strapped to the pannier frame of my old motorbike—happy days!

In complete contrast is the equipment I use these days: thermostatically-controlled electric propagators, accurate to 1°C; soil-warming cables; and fan heaters that blow cold in summer as well as warm in winter—these provide the air circulation that is so vital in our war against mildews. On the subject of air circulation, the automatic opening apparatus for roof vents and louvres are a boon for the absentee gardener during changeable weather.

GARDEN FRAMES

Plastic in all its myriad forms has had its part to play. Bubble plastic can be used for insulation, and garden frames and cloches are all now made of plastic, a boon for ease of maintenance and also for peace of mind where young children and pets are involved.

Woven fleeces are an invaluable aid in protecting crops against both pests and frost. It is astonishing how we managed without them. I remember making many garden frames in the past with timber and bricks, but now I use a row of frames, which are glazed with a rigid plastic box-section material, allowing plenty of light through (so vital in spring). It has a double-glazing effect because of its twin-wall structure, and the framework is all aluminium, this makes them just about maintenance-free, all that you need is a screwdriver.

TOOLS

Basic garden tools have altered very little over the years, although stainless steel is now more widely used. However, power tools have, in my lifetime, advanced out of all recognition. The trend has been to develop bigger, better and quieter models, although I've still never found a quiet shredder. Hedge-cutters, strimmers and mowers are available in a bewildering array of sizes and prices, and these are all aimed to give better results in a shorter time and so give us longer in the deck chair.

It is a fact that the amount of money spent on gardening equipment in this country is the equivalent of every man, woman and child spending £80 per annum, this explains why so much has been invested in developing new and more competitive designs. So shop around and make sure your needs are fully met whatever you purchase.

When considering all the various sundries, I find the new multi-cell trays in a bewildering array of sizes and formats very useful. You can now easily find units for all sizes of seeds, seedlings and cuttings. My only criticism is that the taper and size of all seed-trays and pots should be standardised for ease of both use and stacking, I have a real headache getting a snug fit in my electric propagators.

WOOL: A TRULY ORGANIC PRODUCT

Recently two by-products of the woollen industry have become available for the home gardener. They both merit attention, and as they were previously discarded, it is good to be able to use what was previously treated as a waste product.

'Wulch'

One product is waste wool, which is needle-pressed and dyed a dark brown or black. Sold in rolls, with a thickness reminiscent of carpet underfelt, it is used as a weed suppressant and a water-retaining mulch. Its brand name is 'Wulch'! Lay it on dug and prepared land, and plant shrubs through crosses cut in the material. The 'Wulch' will biodegrade completely in 2–3 years, and in the meantime it will reduce the need for watering, stifle weeds, and, the final benefit of all, in the rotting process it will release fertiliser—mostly nitrogen—into the soil.

Wool-Moss

Recently uproar was caused by thoughtless people stripping moss from various sites in order to line their hanging baskets. A moss substitute is now available, made entirely from waste wool, it is dyed a convincing green/brown, and imitates the appearance of moss perfectly.

SEEDSMEN AND PLANT BREEDERS

Over the last forty years or so many changes have come about. One of the most significant steps forward is the introduction of F1 hybrids. They represent a fantastic development, superseding the old open pollinated strains of yesteryear, with their uniform growth and vigour. Each year new and better strains keep appearing, and sometimes we may feel overwhelmed with choice, and need to exercise some restraint on our purse-strings.

We are all striving for perfection, which is, of course, unobtainable, especially considering the uncertainties of weather and pests, but our industry is certainly not one to rest on its laurels. Modern commercial nurseries have become plant factories replete with the most sophisticated equipment for flow-line production. The process begins with automatic tray and pot fillers and seeding machines and is followed by automatic watering, feeding and ventilation, all of which is computer-controlled. Finally, temperature-controlled vehicles convey the produce to the retailer. Throughout this process, labour requirements are kept to a minimum. The retailer and seedsman can now offer a wide range of plug or mini-plants, often at the same price as the seed! This may well be the way forward for the amateur gardener with limited time or equipment.

Two plants that I am especially keen on at the moment are the *Surfinia* petunias and the trailing antirrhinum *Lampion*. They are both F1 hybrids, trailing in habit, and both are vegetatively propagated. I believe they are here to stay and soon destined to become the two most popular plants for hanging baskets. Even the packaging of seeds has seen dramatic progress. Superseding the old paper packets, the modern foil pack increases the storage life out of all recognition, providing the seal is not broken.

Daffodils have been a particular love of mine, both on a professional and amateur level, and research and development in the UK has remained active. The UK are in fact currently the largest growers of daffodils in the world, and our production even outstrips that of the Dutch. The latest development in daffodil bulb production is a technique known as 'chipping', where the plate of a sound bulb is cut into tiny precise segments (36 to a bulb). They are cultivated under test-tube conditions with a strictly controlled environment, so that after three years each segment has grown into a full bulb—a 36-fold increase! These are easily recognised as they are so precisely round and uniform.

COMPOSTS AND GROWING MEDIUMS

When I first began to deal with seed and potting composts, I remember learning by heart the formula for John Innes composts and John Innes base fertilisers. The internal dimensions of a bushel box (22" x 10" x 10") are indelibly printed on my mind, as every self-respecting apprentice was required to make them. The JI composts were always referred to as 7–3–2 mixes, as the main ingredients are seven parts sterilised loam, three parts peat (sphagnum), and two parts grit sand. All parts were measured by volume, and to each bushel was added four, eight or twelve ounces of John Innes base fertiliser, depending on whether one was making No. 1, 2 or 3 compost.

This formulation, which was devised by the John Innes institute in the 1930s, has stood the test of time, and is still manufactured and used by some stalwarts today. Its decline was principally brought about by the shortage of sterilised loam, and certain unscrupulous dealers tried to cash in by offering an inferior substitute. However today, several leading compost manufacturers have formed an association, their bags are clearly marked and the quality of the product is assured.

Peat composts have won a large share of the market as they are lightweight, sterile and easy to handle, although we are now being urged to conserve peat and seek alternatives. At the time of writing, many substitutes are available and more are being developed. Coir, which is a by-product of the coconut, basically the outer skin or husk, is the one most widely offered. The main problem with it is the need to learn a different watering technique, as the compost can appear dry on the surface, but be moist beneath, and also it runs out of steam, leaving plants requiring liquid feeding as early as four weeks after potting.

Growing mediums constitute a very competitive market at the moment, but one should not always buy the cheapest, as it can prove to be a false economy. There are several additions available for soilless mixes, both peat- and peat-alternative-based. All will increase the price, but can yield much-improved results, particularly vermiculite and perlite, which afford improved drainage and allow the free flow of air—composts must allow the roots to breathe.

Original peat mixes were formulated by the University of California, and hence known as the 'UCL Mix'. Anyone who used these very early peat composts will remember that if one allowed a container of this to dry out, it was a devil of a job to re-introduce water. Scientists subsequently invented what is known as a 'wetting agent', which is now widely used by most of the major compost makers. The other major breakthrough is the use of polymers or 'water-retaining granules', which may already be included in the compost or can be bought in small packs and added at home. These granules can retain, astonishingly, up to 400 times their own weight of water. When dry, they resemble course white sugar, but when water is added they swell to a gelatine-like mass. One teaspoon of these mixed with the compost of a fifteen-inch hanging basket is adequate. Their purpose is to reduce the frequency of watering, which is a great advantage in hanging baskets, containers and window boxes. A further advantage is that when one applies a liquid feed to a container impregnated with these polymers, the feeding period is also extended.

Available to both the professional grower and home gardener is a range of peat-formulated compressed pellets, some encapsulated in a thin nylon mesh, pH adjusted, and pre-fertilised. When soaked in water, they expand to create a mini-growing unit for either cuttings or seeds.

In summary, how do we evaluate all the myriad of growing mediums available and make a choice? My advice is generally to stick with a brand that by experience has yielded good results. However, it is always wise to obtain as much information as possible on new products and be prepared to experiment, albeit on a small scale. With many years' experience of just such trial and error, I can assure readers that the commercial grower does not change his brand of compost lightly, having too much to lose, but will experiment in a small area and in a controlled manner before making any sweeping decisions.

PESTICIDES AND FUNGICIDES

Greenfly

Of every single garden pest,
I think I hate the greenfly best,
My hate for him is stern and strong
I've hated him both loud and long,
Since first I met him in the spring,
I've hated him like anything.

There was one greenfly I recall,
I hated him the most of all,
He sat upon my finest rose,
And put his finger to his nose,
Then sneered and turned away his head,
To bite my rose of royal red.

Next day I noticed, with alarm,
That he had started out to charm,
A lady fly as green in hue,
As all the grass that ever grew.
He wooed, he won; she named the night!
And gave my rose another bite.

Ye gods, quoth I, if this goes on,
Before another week has gone,
These two will propagate their kind,
Until one morning I shall find,
A million greenfly on my roses,
All with their fingers to their noses.

I made a fire, I stoked it hot,
With all the rubbish I had got,
I picked the rose of royal red,
Which should have been their bridal bed,
And on the day the twain were mated
They also were incinerated.

Reginald Parkell

This subject is the proverbial minefield: for experts as well as laymen, and I am hesitant in offering advice. When preparing notes for adult education classes many years ago, I was accustomed to giving 'broad-brush' advice on pesticides, namely: 'If it's above ground, spray it with a DDT mix; if it's a soil-borne pest, use Aldrin

Dust'. Although this advice was given in all good faith and was received wisdom at the time, both substances were subsequently banned due to their persistence in the soil. Fortunately, strict monitoring and testing of chemicals is now a legal requirement.

Many products to which the commercial grower has access are not available to the home gardener for a variety of reasons. Tremendous progress has been made with what are known as 'growth-retardant' agents. This means that flowers can be produced much shorter, so that both wind damage and staking are avoided. Also, when used on hedges and lawns, frequent cutting is reduced: on a commercial project, this is a distinct advantage, as labour is often the largest cost of any enterprise.

Systemic sprays are another recent development, whereby the chemical is absorbed through the leaf pores, and carried by translocation to the main sap stream. When insecticides are presented in this format, the sap is rendered toxic, so when the aphid alights and takes a bite he is in effect committing suicide! The systemic types of weedkillers—Glyphosate-based is the most popular—work by the same principle, i.e. they are taken up by the leaf and transferred to the roots to effect the weed's demise. The strength of this product lies in the fact that it is completely inert when in the soil and only acts on green-leaved plants. However, be careful as it is non-selective, so only spray weeds.

The most important advice I can give on all products designed for pests, weeds or diseases is to read the instructions at least twice before using. Take all precautions and wash out all containers and sprayers very thoroughly. The anti-spray lobbyists would prefer to see all pesticides banned, but I firmly believe a preventative spray is often indicated. Prevention is better than cure, and who wants to eat vegetables after slugs or wireworms have had their share. Besides, 'green' or organic products are available.

Another point I like to reiterate is that, in the same way that the pike in the river usually feeds on the weaker fish, pests and diseases often prey on the less vigorous plants, so we should aim to grow the strongest and best. A big breakthrough—although these have been used for some years for the commercial nurserymen—is the availability of natural predators and nematodes in small packs for home use. By using natural organisms, we introduce 'goodies' to devour the 'baddies'. There are basic guidelines to be observed, namely do not spray or use any smoke-bombs while these are present, and a reasonable temperature is needed to support many of them, so they are not suitable for winter use in a cold greenhouse. Detailed instructions are now widely available, and it's only a matter of time before more pests will be covered by the range offered. The neatness of this method that should be appreciated is that once all the pests have been devoured, your predators will starve. The pests covered by the present range of predators and nematodes is quite impressive, and includes: aphids, caterpillar, mealy bug, red spider mite, scale insects, slugs and snails, white fly, cut worms, and vine weevil. This is quite a wide spectrum, and of course it is a biological control so there are no harmful chemicals to contend with.

From the above, I'm sure you can appreciate the amount of money and effort the horticultural industry is putting into the task of helping us to grow bigger, better and brighter crops. Personally, I am very grateful for their efforts and hope they keep up the good work.

The lacewing a 'goody' in the garden, feeding on aphids.

Where Are We Going?

THE PROGRESS OF GARDENING, both as a hobby and an industry, has been quite phenomenal, and the development of techniques and products continues apace. When I look back to my early years in gardening there are very few aspects that have not undergone radical change, and whilst I avidly read and trial as many new innovations as possible, it is frankly difficult to keep abreast.

PEAT PRODUCTS

Now we have become aware of the need to conserve our dwindling natural resources, I wonder what the future holds for peat products? There are still vast tracts of untapped sites in Russia and the Scandinavian countries, but it seems likely that a recycled compost will eventually prove itself and replace the need for peat.

LABORATORY BREEDING

The seedsmen still keep surprising us by improving on what we thought were the ultimate. 'Micro-propagation', 'cell division', 'test-tube plant division': whatever it is called, great progress is expected in the future, and even today huge strides are being taken in laboratory plant breeding. Soilless cultivation, or 'hydroponics' has been employed with success for many years, and I'm sure current knowledge is only the tip of the iceberg.

CONTAINER WORK

Generally gardens are getting smaller, and it is more common for both partners in a household to work, so containers have boomed in popularity. As mentioned earlier, mini-veg is very much in vogue, and I am convinced it is destined to be further improved and developed. Whatever developments are made, however, nothing will ever equal the taste of fresh produce, and here water-retaining polymers and controlled-release fertilisers have an important part to play. When I started gardening seriously, we used such fertilisers as 'straights' and, for a balanced feed, the well-respected 7–7–7, or as it was known to the layman, 'National Growmore'. These—along with a liberal amount of farmyard manure—all gave us good results, but we never could have imagined that we would be able to buy controlled-release resin-coated compound fertilisers that will go on providing nutrients for two years or more.

POLYTHENE TUNNELS

Poly tunnels are now being made longer-lasting and more attractive in appearance, following years of research and development by the commercial growers: future developments should be worth keeping an eye on. Experiments have also taken place on self-inflating growing structures, which are portable and can be stored compactly when not in use. Solar heat is a subject that I'm sure we will hear a lot of in the not-too-distant future; I personally am very excited by the prospect.

PARASITES AND PREDATORS

Perhaps the fastest progress has been made with the range of parasites and predators now widely available for use as 'pesticides'. They are all carefully tested and monitored and will cut down drastically on the amount of sprays we use. Pest and disease control is by and large a war of attrition: in the last decade I have seen such daunting problems as; *western flower thrip*, *white rust* and, more recently, *black cotton* or *melon aphid* all raise their ugly heads and eventually be defeated by science. The latest problem is the *New Zealand flat worm* which devours the humus-creating earthworms.

THE FUTURE?

Leisure time in this country is definitely on the increase, so I am sure gardening will retain its position as the most popular hobby. Investment in labour-saving devices will therefore continue, so we will be able to spend more time in peaceful reflection of the small oasis of tranquillity and beauty that we and nature together have created.

Another prediction I feel confident enough to make is of the advent of better irrigation and feeding equipment. We now have hydroponic growing systems available and many watering kits, from the simple to the highly sophisticated, including a very efficient system, known as the Bulrush Easigrow. Used with a growbag, it provides up to fourteen days' watering and feeding by capillary action, enabling a gardener to take a break with an easy mind. This system can be used on patios and balconies to grow flowers and vegetables.

At the risk of sounding over-optimistic, I believe the future is very bright for the gardener of today, notwithstanding all our past success and achievements. We will, I am sure, continue to progress as we have done during my forty years of gardening, and we are blessed in the UK with a temperate climate that enables diverse crops to be grown.

I always claim that gardening is 90% common sense and 10% know-how, and I can only hope that this book has helped you along in some way. I first put pen to paper following prompting from various sources, all of whom I trust have not been too disappointed. One of the most rewarding things about writing this was that it brought back a flood of memories from my early days, way back to the days when I became the proud tenant of an allotment myself at the tender age of 21—happy days!.

I close with an extract from one of the most famous British poets, and my favourite verse, which I feel exemplifies the gardener and his garden far better than I ever could.

The Glory of the Garden

Oh, Adam was a gardener and God who made him sees,
That half a proper gardener's work is done upon his knees,
So when your work is finished, you can wash your hands and pray,
For the glory of the garden, that it may not pass away!
And the glory of the garden it shall never pass away!

Rudyard Kipling